D1451752

THE LAND AND PEOPLE
OF FINLAND

THE
LAND AND PEOPLE
OF
FINLAND

BY ERICK BERRY

Portraits of the Nations Series

J. B. LIPPINCOTT COMPANY
PHILADELPHIA & NEW YORK

COPYRIGHT © 1959 BY ALLENA CHAMPLIN BEST
PRINTED IN THE UNITED STATES OF AMERICA
LIBRARY OF CONGRESS CATALOG CARD NUMBER 58-59935

FOURTH IMPRESSION

The author wishes to thank the Finnish Tourist Association for their permission to use the photographs reproduced in this book.

CONTENTS

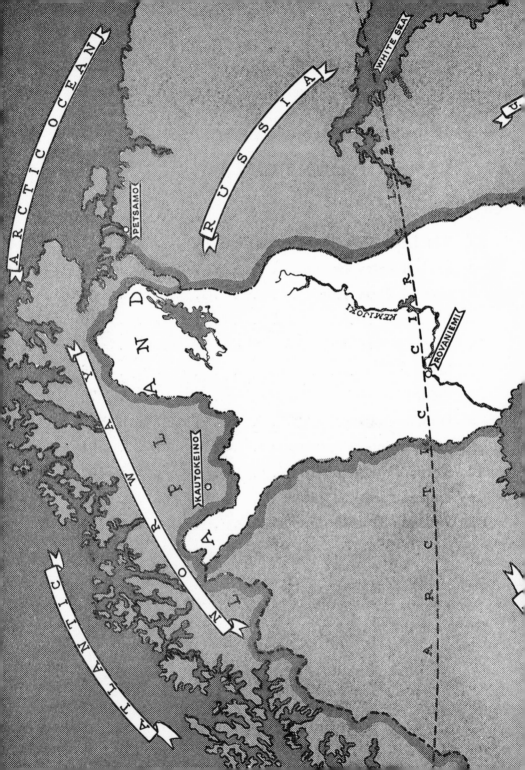

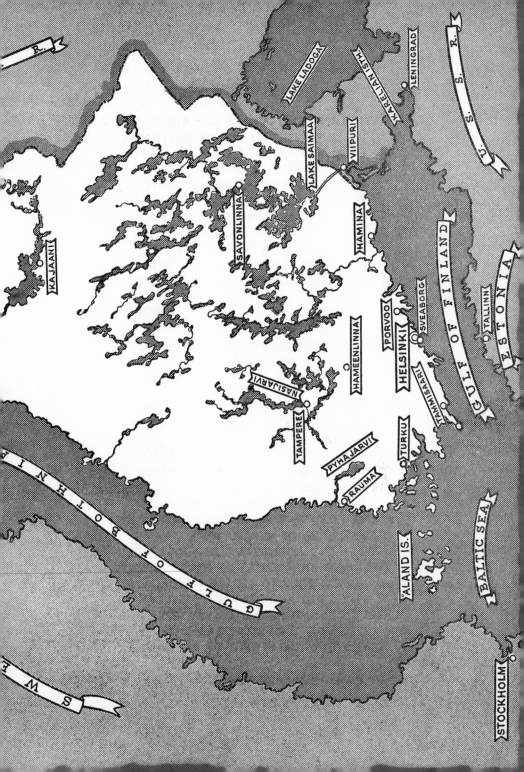

THE LAND AND PEOPLE
OF FINLAND

1

The Land That Rose
Out of the Sea

THE NATIONAL CHARACTERISTIC of the Finnish people can be summed up in one short word. That word is *sisu*.

It is a Finnish word. Sisu has no exact synonym in other languages, perhaps because among other peoples there is no exact counterpart for the quality it denotes. Its meaning is a solid, even stolid, rock-like obstinancy. And from this quality derives the patient endurance and dogged courage on which the Finns pride themselves. This quality of sisu has preserved the Finns as a race through thousands of years of primitive life; it has preserved them through hundreds of years of occupation of their country, first by Sweden, then again and again by Russia, where a more flamboyant gallantry would have surely given way to despair. And it has at last borne them through their long struggle into independence and nationhood.

A whole people does not acquire so striking a trait of character by mere chance; it is a product of both inheritance and environment. The American pioneer, of hardy stock to begin with, was further shaped into tough self-reliance by the dangers and the harshness of his surroundings. The Arab may owe his burning fanaticism to the unforgiving sun beneath which he lives, and his physical endurance to his exacting, barren land. The city dweller, attracted to towns by his ambition, may derive his ever-mounting aspirations from the soaring buildings that surround him and remind him at every turn how man's achievements may dwarf even man himself.

So it has been with the Finns. These people, so stubborn through the centuries in resisting all attempts to change or destroy them, live on a rock formation of the oldest and most obdurate stone in the world. It is as though something of this stubborn, everlasting granite had permeated the soul of the Finn.

The rock base beneath Finland, thinly covered with soil, is part of a great land mass called by geologists the Finno-Scandian shield, the earliest rock formation still to be found on the earth's surface.

For hundreds of thousands of years all northern Europe was covered with a thick layer of ice, miles deep. For tens of thousands of years this icecap slowly melted, then froze again, and again melted and froze. By study of mud and clay strata geologists can trace this grudging recession.

Finally, in the battle between cold and warmth, the warm sun won. About sixteen thousand years ago the glaciers began, for the last time, to recede from southern Sweden and Finland, slowly thereafter creeping northward, sometimes as much as four hundred yards a year.

Yet still there was no Finland. The land itself had yet to be born. The crust of the earth is more or less elastic; pressed down by the enormous weight of ice to the north, its surface bulged elsewhere. And a new land rose slowly out of the Baltic, shedding some of its water, retaining its nearly one hundred thousand lakes. For the first time the land of the Finns emerged, bare and dripping from its long sea bath, ready, when the hour dawned, to take its place in history.

With the retreat of the ice and the development of a warmer,

drier climate, warmer and drier than today, came the willow and
the dwarf birch, came then the wolf and the reindeer. And, some
eight thousand years ago, a tribal nomadic people began to strag-
gle northward across the land bridge on the southeast, now known
as the Karelian Isthmus. It is probable that they came from
somewhere in what is now Russia, somewhere between the Ural
Mountains and the big bend of the Volga River.

For a while they lingered in the land along the Baltic. Then,
as more and more people were thrust out from Asia, by hunger,
by crowding, by ancient feuds between tribes, the first comers,
the reindeer hunters whom we now call Lapps, were driven
further and further north. In their own language Lapp means
"the Banished." The Suomi, the Finns, took over the warmer,
more pleasant land.

Whether the Finns and Lapps were once related is not known;
several thousand years separated their migrations, and when the
Finns did arrive they had in their wanderings picked up a new
way of life and a knowledge of lumbering and agriculture. The
Lapps were still only hunters. The two languages are so distinct
that the two groups are no longer considered part of the same
racial stock, if they ever were.

The Finns belong to what is known as Finno-Ugrian stock.
This means they are loosely related to the Estonians across the
gulf, who called themselves the Baltics, or the Bold-Ones. The
Bold-Ones were a later migration. And even later than these
were the Magyars, of the same stock. They settled down, about
the eighth century A.D., in the plains of Hungary. There is a
language relationship between all these three.

The Finland of today lies one third above the Arctic Circle;
but the warm waters of the Gulf Stream divide, swinging south
into the Baltic, north into the Arctic Ocean, so that some northern
ports such as Petsamo are never icebound, and the country is
much warmer than similar latitudes on our side of the Atlantic.
(Traces of a very primitive culture have been found far north

here, and it is thought that small groups of people, living an
Eskimo-like life, may have survived during the long duration of
the last icecap. But they would not have been Finns.)

All below the Arctic Circle is low, flat country, with no hill
higher than a thousand feet. The retreating Ice Age left behind
over thirty thousand islands and more than sixty thousand lakes,
so that in places more than half the surface of the land is swamp
and lake, bog and marsh. The land, deeply wooded, flashes back
sunlight from thousands of water-mirrors, or absorbs it into the
gloom of the deep evergreen forests. Finland, in fact, means "the
land of fens" or swamps, and the Finns call themselves the Suomi,
suo meaning marsh or bog.

Our first message from ancient Finland, other than the one the
archaeologists and geologists and other scientists can tell us, comes
from Tacitus. In A.D. 98 that old Roman tourist wrote home,
telling of a tribe named the "Suiones" . . . a tribe dwelling in the
far north. "Beyond the Suiones," (the Swedes) he told his friends,
"lies another sea, sluggish and almost motionless, with which the
earth is girdled and bounded. Evidence for this is furnished in
the brilliance of the last rays of the sun, which remains so bright
from his setting to his rising again as to dim the stars. Faith adds
further that the sound of Phoebus Apollo's emergence is audible,
and the forms of his horses visible, with the spikes of his crown.
So far (and here rumor speaks the truth) and so far only, does
Nature penetrate."

The "crown of Apollo" and the "sound of his horse's feet" is
as good an explanation as any for the long-reaching fingers of
the Aurora Borealis and the rustle of their passing.

Tacitus, dropping another picture postcard to his Roman
cousins, also mentions skis, an invention of the Finns, and states
that the people were so swift on these long boards or sticks, that
they could follow a deer and overtake it. The old Latin scholar
got all this by hearsay, of course; he never really traveled north of
the Baltic. His letters home dealt mainly with the customs and

manners of the Germanic tribes, among whom he did stay, and his information regarding the ski-hunters must have come mainly from Germans who had traded for skins and amber with the Finns.

It was a couple of centuries after Tacitus when the Finns began to appear in history. Then they bobbed up among the Goths, those Germanic raiders invading the Roman Empire in the third and fourth centuries. All down through history one has to unravel the Finns from a tangle of Lapps, Swedes, Scandinavians and even, at times, Russians. The Icelandic sagas are as liable to call Lapps, Finns as Finns, Lapps. They were both credited with powers of darkness, with being magicians, and worse. Later, when Finland became a duchy of Sweden, Sweden claimed, for herself any men of genius or ability that Finland might possess, such as the poet Runeberg. And still later, when in modern times Russia took over Finland and made her a duchy of Russia, she also, Russian-like, claimed Finland's men of genius for her own—such as Sibelius.

But stubbornly, throughout all this long period, the Finns retained their own character, their sisu. Though they came originally from the East they do not consider themselves related in any way to the Eastern peoples. Their faces, their future, are turned toward the West. Neither do they wish to be considered Scandinavian. Though the Gulf of Bothnia separates them from Sweden, it is difficult not to see them, as on the map, part of the three great northern countries of the Scandinavian Peninsula since they are linked so closely to Lapland, which is common to all. No, the Finns want to be thought of as Finns only; Finnish through and through. An obstinate people!

The early colonists from Asia were hunters and fishers, though they had begun to raise a few crops. They found the bogs and lakes and shores ideal for their way of life, and for the skillful shipbuilding for which later they became famous. In their religion they were what is called shamanists; they believed in personal and nature gods, much as our American Indians did.

Theirs was a strange lonely life, which led to the development of strong introvert characteristics. Settlements were small and widely separated, the countryside an endless expanse of bog and lake and dark forests, the dark brooding winters long and snow-bound, with the Northern Lights, mysterious and awe-inspiring, crackling and flickering across the skies. No wonder that magic and superstition were inbred in these people, and that their worship, or at least propitiation of the Forces of Evil, lasted long after they had accepted Christianity.

By the beginning of the eighth century there were three settled districts in Finland: Suomi in the southwest, which eventually gave its name to the whole people; Hame in the center of the country; and Karelia in the southeast. Northward was still un-settled wasteland, deep pine forests, over which wandered the banished Lapps and their reindeer.

It is probable that there was no sharp change from hunting to nomad-pastoral, to settled-pastoral and to the agricultural way of life, but that these overlapped, as they did in our pioneer days, when a man farmed in summer and hunted and trapped in winter. Well into the Middle Ages the furs and skins of Finland were a large part of Swedish exports.

With each change in the way of earning a livelihood came the usual slow change in social organization. Among nomad hunters and herders the accent is on the family tie, extending to a clan organization of related families. With permanent settlement a family's link with relatives in other villages weakens and gives place to dependence upon neighbors in the same village, though they may be unrelated by blood. Slowly, and not uniformly, throughout the land of the Finns, the primitive clan organization was replaced by territorial rule. Government by the most power-ful man in the village, advised by his neighbors, differs in size, not in system, from national government by presidents and kings with their legislative bodies.

But seasons were very short, the soil thin and poor, the isolated settlements separated by vast wastelands. In such circumstances people do not grow prosperous, nor do they easily develop an advanced type of civilization with a strong central government and a sense of nationhood. Not a very bright prospect, one feels, for the future of a small people surrounded by richer, more numerous races on east and west and south, with only the desolate snowy wastes to the north. But the Finns had their sisu, their stolid endurance, and their national purpose.

Though history may seem to stand still, the evolution of a people continues. For lack of written records or enduring artifacts it is difficult to form a picture of the early stages of Finnish culture, when it occupied a position between that of the Lapps of today and the Finns of today, but the social patterns of people who have passed through the same stages in more recent times afford some clues.

Caution is indicated when seeking to find the Finnish ways mirrored in those of the Swedes or Norwegians, as allowance must be made for all-important religious differences. As the Norse *Heimskringla* reports, the early Norsemen passed through successive stages of ancestor worship and Odin worship before attaining to Christianity. As the Finnish *Kalevala* shows, the Finns remained animists up to the time of their tardy and reluctant conversion to Christianity.

Both ancestor worship and the Odin cult assume the existence of higher and more powerful beings, who must, to a greater or lesser extent, be served and obeyed. Priests exert some form of authority in the name of these powers, prescribing and enforcing worship and tribute. Such authority is gradually assumed by the secular rulers, sometimes easily, sometimes only after centuries of strife between the lay and the spiritual power, which may culminate in the well-known conflicts between cardinals and chancellors and even between kings and popes.

But the Finns had no tradition of obedience to any superior gods or priests to prepare their minds for lay rule. Their shamanistic cult was almost pure animism, and its adepts were more what we would consider medicomagicians than priests. They could, they believed, sway the forces of nature by secret means and for adequate fees; but they neither organized nor were organized; neither obeyed superior shamans—for they recognized none as such—nor exacted obedience.

Animism, as we shall see later, is the most classless of beliefs, conceding something like a soul to all living animals, and even to plants and trees and rocks and water.

Social organization, though delayed by the animistic cult, was inevitable. With the abandonment of pastoral life and the growth of agricultural settlement, arose the inevitable land disputes. Customs, no doubt differing from lawgiver to lawgiver and village to village, became established as to land tenure, damage by livestock (though the Finns have always practiced mixed farming) and whether beasts should be fenced in or fenced out.

When people develop agriculture and can live in closer communities, they meet more often and consequently offend each other more often by word or blow, and intervention and arbitration establishes a code of conduct. Unfortunately, justice was rendered orally, and we have no record of this slow development of a common law.

To round out our picture of the unrecorded life of the day we must envision the individual as well as his civic organization making his own slow but steady progress. Trial and error, stimulated by the growth of population, led as always to minor improvements in farming. The abandonment of nomad life allowed more tools to be accumulated than had been possible when a man had to carry them with him wherever he went or throw them away after use. Crafts were developed.

They also developed special skills. For instance, they felled trees and fitted the interlocking logs into strong walls, like our log cabins, leaving a single smokehole in the roof. This is a remarkable invention, which our Pilgrim Fathers and earliest settlers knew nothing of. In principle it is the same as dovetailing the corners of a box, to make them far stronger than if just nailed together. The roofing was of birch bark, the only material available, but easily come by in any birch forest. Over this water-proof roofing was laid thick, close-fitting turf, to keep out the bitter cold. House insulation, hundreds of years before anyone else thought of it!

Inside, the single room showed only bare unplastered log walls, a very high lintel to keep out drifting snow, and over which one one must step to the earth-floored or, later, stone-floored living quarters. There were bunks for the master and mistress, sometimes a gallery in which the children slept, and a central fire over which hung a gigantic kettle which was swung on a long pole from one side of the room. Such houses were almost standard all over Scandinavia, and it was in such crude quarters that the early Viking raiders were born, though later they lived, for their period, in considerable luxury.

From birchbark these early Finns made shoes, tents, leggings, baskets, plates and platters, boats . . . our American Indian was was not the only experimeter to set forth in frail birch bark canoes. And they were such skilled trappers as to find ready sale for their goods in Fresia—now Holland—at that time and for centuries the clearing house for furs and skins for all Europe.

There is a record in Norwegian history of the "Sea-Finns." This group, carpenters and shipwrights, came to settle, or at least to work for part of the year, along the Norwegian fjords, then thickly forested. They were specialized craftsmen, living entirely by their shipbuilding. Even as early as the Viking days these Sea-Finns never went to sea, but were hired for their skill on dry land; and were especially valuable to the Norse Vikings at a time when the looting and plundering of monasteries along the Irish and English coasts were of far more profit than the building of ships. Hiring carpenters to build the longboats saved valuable time.

This trade lasted from the Iron Age well down into the eighteenth century. In the sagas there is mention of such a commissioned ship being built, in 1138, for a sea king by a "Lapp"— Lapp and Finn being interchangeable. "There were twelve oars to a side and the knees were of willow."

The Viking ships were largely of oak. There is today little oak in Norway, and there was probably none in Finland even then. It may be that the chance of building with oak was what drew the Finns to Norway. There they settled in their own villages and "paid the sheriff a boat a year for tithe on their industry."

These ship carpenters were even then conscientious craftsmen. In the sagas is mention of a longboat, nearly completed; just before her launching it was discovered that all her timbers had been scored again and again with deep cuts. When investigation was made the crime was pinned on a single carpenter. His punishment was to plane out the scars. Gladly he consented to shave down the strakes and rebuild the craft; he had been convinced from the beginning that the planking was far too heavy, and had made the cuts in order to convince the owners of the fact.

Here was a real craftsman, who would risk his life rather than produce a botched job. No wonder those sea wolves, the Vikings, could voyage as far as Greenland, or south to Constantinople, in their longships. The ships were put together with the delicacy of violins. And the Finns were among their master craftsmen.

Nor were the Finns all peaceful craftsmen. They did a tidy little bit of sea-raiding on their own. Mostly they raided along the eastern and southern coast of Sweden, returning home with their loot. By the twelfth century they had grown to be such a nuisance that Eric IX of Sweden decided to put a stop to these heathen practices. Having been baptized himself he sent a group of warriors on what he called a "crusade." They were to conquer Finland; they were also to turn the Finns into good, non-raiding Christians—like himself.

Having achieved his aim, as he thought, he left behind Henry, bishop of Uppsala, thought to be an Englishman—also claimed by Scotland. Henry was to complete the forced conversion of the Finns. But the heathen refused to accept him: they clung to their shamans and their old dark magic. And they murdered the good bishop. Later they made up for this by canonizing him, and today he is Saint Henry, the patron Saint of Finland.

Other priests were dispatched from Sweden, and for a time these obstinate Finns did a brisk trade in enslaved missionaries. A good strong Christian missionary, obedient and submissive, was worth as much as a couple of good bulls. Then, with over-production, the market took a slump, the pagan Finns became impatient and began to hang bishops on trees, for target practice, and as a blunt hint that they were not yet ready to accept the new religion.

It was early in the thirteenth century when another Englishman, willing to demonstrate that he would be as obstinate as any Finn, brought in more priests and a goodly company of warriors. His name was Thomas, and this time the Finns accepted his preaching. He was in fact so astoundingly successful that, being a strong Papist, he nearly succeeded in detaching Finland from Sweden and making it into a province subject directly to Rome and the pope.

Sweden did not then colonize Finland. At that time she was herself too underpopulated to need more land or to spare settlers. But a few of the Swedish nobility took up big estates in the country, especially along the Gulf of Bothnia. By 1362 Finland had become a duchy of Sweden, with the right of any other of the Swedish provinces to send a delegation to the capital to help elect a king.

Sweden brought no great oppression to her duchy; and it was due to her later colonization that Finland escaped being conquered by the German Knights of the Sword, who enslaved the less fortunate Baltic states to the south. It was also due to Swedish strength that Finland escaped being overwhelmed by the Tartars, the conquerors of Novgorod and the founders of modern Russia.

With the Swedish and Russian nutcrackers to west and east, it is a wonder that little Finland survived. The answer begins gradually to appear. Finland was too hard a nut to crack. She was made of obdurate Finnish granite.

2

Finland Faces Sweden

THE TRACING of prehistory, that is, history before there were any archives or written records, is a tricky business. No striking personalities, no Charlemagnes or Napoleons or George Washingtons step forward out of the fog of the past to stride the stage in a blaze of legends; there exists no eyewitness accounts of great battles fought and won, or lost, or Magna Cartas signed or cherry trees hacked down, to assist the writer in his search for local color. We know, by inference, that there were such personalities and such sweeping events, and it would be exciting to discover first-hand accounts of the poisoning of Eric XIV in his gloomy cell in Turku Castle, or the flight and hiding of Gustavus Vasa as he strove to raise an army against the tyrant Danes. But no such records exist. We only know that, for over seven hundred years, the history of Finland was largely the history of Sweden also. For all that time the two countries were interwoven beyond disentangling, and we must deal with the duchy of Finland as a province, almost, of Sweden. Many of Sweden's heroes and outstanding personalities were actually Finns as much as Swedes. Some of them may even have been Lapps.

Though Finland is not geographically part of the great Scandinavian Peninsula and prefers not to be called Scandinavian, it is difficult to separate her completely from her sister countries. She was even, for a time, politically a part of Denmark, since from 1397 to 1521 Sweden was herself ruled by a Danish king, and Finland a duchy of Sweden. During this period there was a long struggle between one Swedish province and another, but no one of them was as yet sufficiently strong to impose its choice of a king upon the others, or to lead the country to break loose from Denmark.

This lack of a leader also held back the development of the country considerably. Sweden lay on the outer edge of Europe's cultural growth; Finland was still further away. She could be approached only by way of the pirate-infested Baltic, and it was only along her extreme southern and western coast that Sweden's, and hence Europe's, influence penetrated.

It has been judged that, in 1600, Sweden's economic level was about that of France or England in the year 1000. That means that at a time when England had known Langland and Chaucer and Shakespeare, Elizabeth and Henry the Eighth and the break with the Catholic Church, Sweden was still back in the time of Alfred the Great, and almost as far back as Charlemagne. She still traded in barter. Taxes and salaries and even interest on loans were all paid in commodities. Right down to the end of the eighteenth century this backward system of barter, without money, still prevailed, as in some New England towns where the parson and the schoolteacher were paid in fuel and foodstuffs, rather than in cash.

On the other hand, and to their advantage, both Sweden and Finland escaped the crippling power of the European feudal system, which was little short of slavery. Even in the Middle Ages Sweden was in a way a democracy and the peasant, never held in serfdom, was an important part of the population. By the end of the Middle Ages the class of free peasant farm owners was large enough to tip the scale in the struggle between the nobility and the monarchy.

Also this was still a rural country; an economy and a pattern of life that still persists today. There were no great powerful cities such as Rome, Venice, Paris and London, with their own laws and overlords, their great merchants and middle-class rulers. As a result, with no middle class of any importance, Sweden's peasants supported her monarch, and for several hundred years the king turned to his free landholding peasants when he wished backing on any point of importance, whether war with another country, or internal strife against the arrogance of the nobility. This would have been unthinkable, even fantastic, in France, in Italy or in Germany of the same period.

Frequently in Finland today you will see the insignia of the Three Crowns. They appear carved above an old stone doorway, or as the name of a modern restaurant, or on a flag fluttering from a window. The Three Crowns date back to the short period between 1388 and 1412, when for a time all three Scandinavian countries were united under one ruler. This also included Finland.

The ruler was a woman, Queen Margaret of Norway. She governed Norway by right of marriage to the king, who had died; she ruled Denmark by right of inheritance from her father. Sweden, suffering under the unpopular Albert of Mecklenburg, growing jealous of this German invasion and resentful of foreign taxes, turned to Norway and to Margaret for relief.

So in 1388 Margaret was elected Sovereign Lady and Ruler. It was her plan to unite the three kingdoms and the three crowns into one whole. Unfortunately Albert decided to fight for his rights. The war that followed lasted seven long and bloody years and ended only with the exhaustion of both sides. But Albert withdrew, back into Europe.

When Margaret died she left no lawful heir to the Three Crowns; only a nephew whom she had renamed Eric and appointed as her successor. He was no more popular than Albert had been and, deposed, was banished to the Island of Gotland. For a time Duke Christopher of Denmark took over the Three

Crowns and there was peace until 1448, when he too died, without an heir. Again the three countries were thrown into confusion: each of the three elected a ruler from the nobility, each of the three was willing to fight to back its choice. In all this Finland, as usual, was involved. She often furnished up to one-third of the troops; her men were drawn from farm and forest to fight on land and sea. Yet no matter which side was victorious, Finland won nothing for herself.

In spite of all this carnage the peasants of Sweden never lost their freedom, never fled to the protection and tyranny of walled cities. The face of the countryside remained unchanged, dotted by village communities dating back a thousand years. Dairy farming, characteristic of independent freedom-loving people from Switzerland to New England, was the general practice. The exports tell us this, for Sweden's main commodity was butter, which comprised a quarter of her foreign trade.

Butter—portable, easily measured, more or less uniform by nature and much in demand—was a convenient substitute for money. It had other uses too, as we learn in the collection of Finnish runes called the *Kalevala,* where the beautiful heroine Aino is urged by her mother:

> Eat, a whole year long, fresh butter
> That your form may grow more rounded.
> Eat thou pork the second season
> That your form may grow more charming.
> And the third year eat thou cream cakes,
> That thou may become more lovely.

Finland liked them plump in those days!

We also know from the records that in 1260 Finland paid half her taxes in butter, and by 1560 half Finland's export, to Holland, Danzig, Lubeck and, of all places, Denmark—today the strongest dairying country in Europe—was butter. This shows us that, in spite of wars, in Finland and in the northern wastes of Sweden, new villages were being founded, forest land was being cleared and settled, and both countries were gradually widening their boundaries.

Then the Danish king, Christian II, invaded Sweden and in 1520 ordered a massacre known in history as the Stockholm Bloodbath. This for a time seemed to wipe out all opposition. No leaders were left; nobles had been slaughtered, even churchmen had been dragged off to Denmark. Among the nobles held as hostage was a young and charming Swede named Gustav Eriksson Vasa.

In him Sweden at last found a leader. It took a long time, however. He managed to make his escape and, disguised as a cowhand, sought refuge in Lübeck. The Danes traced him there and demanded his extradition. But Lübeck refused to surrender him, her citizens even helped him make his way back to Sweden, where in May 1520 he landed near Kalmar. There he learned of the capture of his sister and mother by the Danes, and the death of his brother-in-law and father.

Gustav's youth was against him, but he had a burning thirst for revenge, a gift for oratory and a feeling that King Christian was beginning to overreach himself.

Stealthily he made his way northward to the province of Dalarna, where he began to raise his first troops. The young fugitive, in his round felt hat and peasant garb, is today such a part of legend that it is as difficult to separate truth from fiction, as in the case of that other romantic national fugitive, Bonnie Prince Charlie. For months—pursued by the king's men—Gustav fled from place to place, inciting the peasants to revolt against the foreign monarch, talking to the burgesses, to the nobility. By January of the following year, 1521, his name had reached the ears of the Danish king.

The revolt in Sweden was soon in full swing. Though Gustav began with neither arms nor money, one province after another came to his aid. By June of 1523 Christian had been driven out of Sweden and Gustav Vasa was elected king. He was the founder of the Vasa line, and was the first to proclaim a hereditary monarchy to safeguard any further claims by Denmark to the Swedish throne.

This was a momentous period. America had been recently discovered by Columbus, Magellan was making his first circumnavigation of the globe; and in Germany a controversy was raging round the new doctrines of Martin Luther. The medieval world was falling into ruins.

A portrait of Gustav Vasa, painted later in life, shows his forceful character but gives us no hint of his youthful charm. We see a portly man, with a bowl haircut and bangs, wearing the flat-topped velvet cap we see in pictures of Henry VIII: in fact the heavily jeweled garments, the air of assured arrogance, the hand on sword, are very similar. But Sweden's king wears a full beard, and the extremely long nose and pouched eyes are characteristically Swedish. There is a further similarity. Gustav, like Henry, was reported a "gay and witty companion" with an astounding memory and a prodigious capacity for work.

It was during the reign of Vasa that Sweden broke with the Catholic Church, as England did during the reign of Henry VIII. But Gustav, unlike his fellow monarch, left a son to carry on the line.

This king was Eric XIV. He began his reign well enough, with a splendid coronation, to which came people from all corners of his kingdom. There were even Lapps and reindeer among them: Lapps no doubt in their white deerskin garments gaily embroidered in the colors and patterns of the Northern Lights and wearing their caps with the gigantic red wool pompons; reindeer in their red leather harness and silver bells. It was Sweden's first great coronation.

In his portrait we see a long lean ascetic face, unstable and ailing, as though he had been a delicate, indulged child. His forehead, which might tell us more of him, is hidden by the black velvet cap with earflaps which was the fashion of the day, and which the drafty stone castle halls demanded, if kings and lesser fry were not to suffer from stiff neck or a cold in the head. He wears a soft drooping mustache and drooping beard, and one can see no resemblance to the bluff, hearty and extremely popular Gustav Vasa.

Eric sought his new queen pretty thoroughly through the various courts of Europe, and with scant success. He sent costly courting gifts to Elizabeth of England . . . as what monarch did not? Then he had a try for Mary Stuart of Scotland. And again no luck. In the end he married a lovely and patient Finnish girl named Karin Mansdotter, Katherine, Daughter of the Moon, who had been his mistress for many years and who bore him two children.

Gustav's genius had, in his son, turned to willful eccentricity: Eric's instability developed into downright insanity. He imprisoned his younger brother Johan in Turku Castle in Finland and even made an attempt on his life. Johan, at this time, was duke of Finland, for the duchy of Finland was, to Sweden, much as Wales was to Great Britain, the duke of Finland always being the Heir apparent as is the Prince of Wales to the English throne.

There followed more crippling wars between Denmark and Sweden for which, as always, Finland furnished men-at-arms. At last, when Eric almost playfully began to kill off the nobles who had been his main support, they joined with Johan and had him deposed. Eric spent the next nine years a prisoner in his small dark cell in Turku, Finland. It can be seen there today, much as when he dwelt in it.

During most of the period between 1570 and 1809 Sweden not only fought her old enemy Denmark and the German states, but she carried on a constant series of wars with Russia. There were, in this period, five wars, lasting a total of sixty years, between Russia and her western neighbor, with Finland serving as the unlucky battleground. Even when Charles XII of Sweden, at the beginning of the eighteenth century, was leading his victorious armies into the heart of Russia, Peter the Great swept down on Finland and from Lake Ladoga in the east to the Gulf of Bothnia in the west laid waste the land. Finnish historians call this the Great Wrath.

For four centuries Finland had no more than a single generation of peace. Is it any wonder that hatred of Russia became an ingrained part of the Finnish character?

Many Finns sought a home in other countries, and among the first settlers in America there were as many Finns as there were Dutch along the Hudson, or English in the Bay Colony. It was mainly Finns who cleared the forest for the site of a future Philadelphia. And it was either Swedes or Finns who passed on to the English settlers their own home-country method of fitting horizontally laid logs together, in the pattern that is now known as the New England log cabin. Earlier log cabins, built by the English, planted the logs stockade fashion, upright in the ground.

John Morton, one signer of the Declaration, was of Finnish descent. But by his time the earlier wave of immigrants had spread out along the Delaware and become true Americans, largely farmers. When, in 1850, a second wave of them began to arrive from Finland they were largely lumbermen and miners. They sought land further west, rocky country that seemed to them more homelike than the peaceful rolling valley along the Delaware.

But Finland did not serve solely as a prison for Sweden's mad monarchs, nor wholly as a source of cannon fodder. Her university at Turku (Abo) was an early rival of the famous University of Uppsala in Sweden; and Abo's library was considered the finest in all the north country. Her conquest by Sweden brought her many benefits: it made her first a Catholic country, and later a Lutheran one. It rapidly developed her exports and her national economy.

Not least of the benefits, this collaboration of Swedes and Finns along her west coast gave birth to a new mixed race. The intermarriage of the long-limbed extrovert and adaptable Swedes with the phlegmatic, stubborn, stocky and introvert Finns, gave Finland some of her finest men. Among these Swedo-Finns were many of the leaders in the nationalist movement in centuries to come. The Swedes, separated by the Gulf of Bothnia from their mother country, became landowners in Finland, and though it was many generations before they learned to speak her language, they became leaders in her cultural, political and commercial life, and in the end greatly added to the wealth that Sweden had bestowed on her duchy.

The obstinate centuries-long struggle, at heavy cost in lives and property, had done more than preserve a small people from obliteration. In the end it converted the Swedes of Finland into Finnish patriots. But this remarkable result lay far in the future and many wars raged, like stormy seas, between.

3

Finland Faces Russia

HOME RULE for Finland might never have occurred
had it not been for one of those odd accidents in history that so
often prove overwhelmingly important. The country became a
pawn in Napoleon's campaign against the rest of the world. The
emperor made an alliance with Denmark by which he hoped to
close the Baltic to British trade. He attempted to do the same
with Sweden.

But Gustav IV of Sweden had a deep personal hatred of Napoleon. Sweden also considered that the Baltic Sea was her own,
to do with as she chose. She refused his offer. Then Napoleon
made advances to Russia. He persuaded Alexander I to declare
war on Sweden; probably not a very difficult thing to do, since
Russia and Sweden had been at war, off and on, for centuries. At
the same time Sweden was to be attacked by Denmark. Little Finland was to be Russia's prize in this treachery.

So, under a flag of truce and with no excuse whatever, in Feb-
ruary 1808, Russians marched into Finland. The defenders had
good troops and held excellent positions, but treachery and in-
competence tossed away these two advantages and, with the coming of summer, Sweden sent no further help. Sveaborg (now
Suomenlinna), the fortress of Helsinki, surrendered without a shot
being fired, and when the Russian troops entered Turku they

were met with a civic reception! The Swedo-Finns had betrayed both Sweden and Finland.

For centuries the Finns had loathed the Slavs and had fought them, so now, though the war was over so far as their generals were concerned, the Finnish peasants, inflamed by a thousand years of accumulated bitterness, turned and fought. Fighting with the guerrilla methods which best suited the heavily forested country, and led by three excellent generals of their own choice, they held out for five months, though with an army of only 12,000 against one of 55,000. For the eighteen months that followed, though they were losing, Finland still held on. Then Sweden, signing a treaty with Russia, handed over Finland. This was in September, 1809.

But Alexander I, much to the surprise of Finland, had already made his peace with that country. In March, 1809, at Porvoo, six months before the fighting ceased, he offered them a greater degree of self-government than they had ever enjoyed under Sweden's rule.

Today, despite all their bitterness against the Slav, the Finns revere the memory of Alexander, whose statue, the only statue of a Russian in all the country, still stands in Suurtori Square in the center of Helsinki.

So generous were the terms of this Tsar of all the Russias, that Finland at last seemed to be on her own. She was now a Russian duchy, but her farmers, as opposed to the Russian serfs, were free; they were excused from military service, they had their own legislature with their own laws, courts, schools and university. They were given the military protection of a great country. And in 1812 Alexander generously returned to Finland an ancient province of Viipuri, with its outlet to the Baltic, and its wealthy Greek Orthodox monastery. Now Finland should be free, and happy.

But she was not. It is possible that Alexander had thought that he was freeing a mere province of Sweden, for when he had visited the country he had heard only Swedish spoken; the culture and the church were almost wholly Swedish. What Russia had done was to hand the country over to its former landowners, the Swedo-Finns. The gulf between the two peoples caused increasing hostility; two bitterly opposed parties were forming themselves, each speaking its own language, each wanting to rule. Their only point in common was their hatred of Russia.

For both parties were keenly conscious of the rift between East and West. Both Swedes and Finns considered themselves part of Western civilization; Russia, to them, belonged to the hated East.

Yet the country prospered. The Industrial Revolution began to take effect; the first great canal, between Lake Saimaa and the Gulf of Finland, was opened, the first railroad was built.

The Finns began to feel economically independent; their tar boats down the Kemijoki exported "Stockholm tar" to shipyards all over the world, their log rafts swirled down a dozen rivers to the gulf. Farmers who had scraped a bare living from the thin soil began to cut and sell their lumber, the labor movement took on impetus, and Finland exported butter by the ton.

But with the coming of Nicholas II to the Russian throne all this was altered. Russia began to ask herself what good she was getting out of Finland. Why were the Finns so free that they were even able to set a tax on Russian imports? Why did they pay no taxes to Russia? Why did they furnish no soldiers for the Russian army?

In 1899, the short period of peace and security came to an end. A new military law, practically amalgamating the Finnish with the Russian military forces, was put into effect. She was no longer to be ruled by her own laws, but by the laws of Russia. Russian officials were foisted upon her; Russian was to be taught in her schools, by force if necessary; and General Bobrikov was appointed governor general, with full powers of dictatorship. Finland was no longer a free country.

Protests against this tyranny came from all over Finland; indeed from many parts of the world. The Tsar refused to look at the petition, or to grant audience to a committee of distinguished scholars and statesmen who came to lay their claims before him. His reply was to increase the pressure on Finland. Russian was henceforth to be the language not only of the higher courts but of the civil courts, and the laws were to be printed in that language. The press was muzzled. A secret police system was installed with spies everywhere. But the whole Russian pattern, whether Imperial or Soviet, is by now so familiar to us that it hardly needs to be underlined.

The result was unexpected. It began to weld the two Finnish groups, Swedo-Finns and Finnish, into one solid mass of national resistance, of sisu. The hatred of Bobrikov was so great that between Russian and Finn there was almost no communication; no Russian was invited to set foot inside a Finnish household, no Russian was received socially, no matter what his title or what his class. Then one day a somewhat shy young government clerk shot the governor general dead in the street and turned the gun on himself. In his pocket was found a letter addressed to the Tsar, in which he stated that no Finnish group was behind his deed, and he and he alone was to blame. He was of the opinion that Nicholas did not know or understand the tyranny being applied to Finland, and that the death of the governor would bring it to his notice and it would cease.

But the effect was slight so far as Russia was concerned. Though the Tsar promised reforms, none was forthcoming, and in June, 1910, an edict was issued turning Finland into a mere province of Russia. The Tsar and the Russian Duma were given sole rights to pass her laws: there was to be no further representation by Finland, neither in fact nor in pretense.

What would happen next? Finland was determined, more determined than ever, to have her freedom. But she could not fight Russia singlehanded . . . though she was almost prepared to. Then, in August 1914, the whole of Europe plunged into war.

Finland's opportunity to realize the aim that she had held to for hundreds of years came suddenly, almost unexpectedly. Russia, concerned with her own revolution and the overthrow of the tsarist regime, was in too chaotic a state to control her neighbor; and on December 6, 1917, the parliament in Helsinki issued a declaration of independence. That day is still celebrated all over the country, as is our Fourth of July in the U.S.A.

But Finland was overrun with Russian soldiers, undisciplined, without officers, often without food or shelter. There was much shooting and looting; chaos reigned. The Socialists seized power and set up their own government. The legal government withdrew north, and under Carl Gustav Mannerheim the White army was formed. It received help and arms from Germany. The Reds were being aided by Russia and there were many Russians among them. It was not until 1918 that the Reds were defeated, and the Whites came into power. In October 1920 a formal peace was signed—the Treaty of Dorpat—and for the first time in her history, and the last time to date, Finland held all the territory due her, from the valuable ice-free port of Petsamo on the Arctic Ocean, and the nickel mines so important in both war and peace, south to her old province of Karelia; that province which stretches along the Karelian Isthmus on the Gulf of Finland to within a few miles of Petrograd.

For a few years Finland lived in peace and considerable prosperity. Then came the Second World War.

It was during this breathing space that Finland, now independent and bound together by past suffering and pride in her achievement, could cease watching her frontiers with anxious eyes and turn her attention inward upon her people and the improvement of their standard of living.

Finland's post-war poverty stimulated the growth of a means of collection and distribution of goods which would reduce the toll of national wealth taken by the unproductive middleman, thus ensuring higher prices to the producer and lower prices to the consumer. This method is known as the co-operative.

There is nothing new in communal labor or communal ownership. In the very dawn of history hunters banded together for game drives and tribal fights, and neighbors ever since have joined forces in jobs which were beyond the strength of single individuals. Nor is joint ownership new; ships and trading ventures have been owned in shares; and undivided grazing ground called a common was characteristic of early New England, and of many primitive villages. When early in this century Finnish farmers began to form small groups to buy imported feed in wholesale lots at wholesale prices, or jointly to purchase a pedigree bull to grade up their livestock, they were breaking no new ground.

Much earlier than this Finnish reformers had tried to arouse national interest in joint buying and selling and collective ownership. But sisu can take the form of dogged progress over all obstacles, or equally obstinate refusal to budge on the grounds that "what was good enough for granddad is good enough for me." Slowly, however, the idea took on, and in 1899 the first consumer's co-op was established in Helsinki. It was not successful, for Russia, then Finland's overlord, disapproved, and the peasants were in no position to persist.

Yet the need was there, and in 1901 three co-ops were established, and this time throve. After the First World War, the tentative experiment became a necessity if the standard of living was to be maintained. After the Second World War, economic chaos left a gap which could only be filled by the extension of the co-operative movement in every imaginable form.

In Finland the co-operative has now developed far beyond the economic experiment, or the emergency stopgap. It is a way of life, a pattern of thought, almost a religion; it reaches out into every corner of the nation and permeates all activity. Through it the housewife learns her domestic science, the farmer hears of new machinery and improvements in livestock-raising or book-keeping. It has become far more than joint stockholding. It has developed into a flexible organizational unit, reaching out like a benign octopus into anything from education to credit banking.

Many of the city apartments are co-ops—in Helsinki, in Tampere, Turku and elsewhere—jointly owned and operated by all the tenants. We have a similar arrangement in some cities in the United States. Many of the factories are co-ops, as are stores, wholesale houses and banks, throughout the country. Without these societies it is doubtful if the people of Finland would ever have emerged from a poverty-stricken and backward peasantry.

Of all the northern countries Finland is now the most advanced in the development of the co-ops. Nearly every family in the country belongs to at least one, and total membership, in a country of four millions, is more than a million and a half—surely a formidable achievement in a little over fifty years.

It is tempting to try to guess the future course of the co-operative movement in relation to national government. Organization on the clan system was replaced, when agriculture changed the way of life, by villages, groups of villages and other territorial units. The growth of manufacturing, transportation and the increasing complexity of a nation's economic system may now be leading to a third change, in the form as well as the life of the Finnish people.

The delegate to a central government from a territorial unit can no longer speak with a sure voice in the interest of all his constituency, for the people whom he represents have no common pattern of life and uniform needs, as they had when all were farmers. A majority in one district can brief their elected representative and make their wishes known, but a greater number of people, if spread as minorities through several electoral districts, have no representation in the national government, and none to safeguard their rights and interests. The trade and craft guilds in the olden days could make their wishes known in the same way that organized labor does today, beyond the confines of electoral districts. But these represent only producers, not the equally important consumers in a nation. Co-ops make no such dangerous distinction, for they represent the consumer as much as the producer, and have as much interest in keeping prices down as keeping wages up. Surely a healthy thing, if a nation's economy is to be stable, and inflation and deflation are to be avoided.

The Finnish co-operative, prides itself as a rule on being nonpolitical. In other words, it neither threatens nor promises. But it can make known, in no uncertain voice, the wishes of small minorities, or of the politically unorganized housewife.

4

It's Magic!

ALL DOWN THROUGH the ages the Lapps and the Finns —the two being indistinguishable in the minds of the early historians—had a reputation for great skill with black magic. Any account of Finland would be incomplete without some mention of this.

In the *Heimskringla, The Lives of the Norse Kings,* as recounted by Snorri Sturluson in the thirteenth century, we learn of a chief who ordered that a Lapp be brought to him, and that the man be tortured until he cast an evil spell on the chief's enemy. This the Lapp accomplished, but then escaped, to cast backward a spell on the chief, so that the man was shortly drowned.

In this tale, as in many others like it, Lapp and Finn seem interchangeable; sometimes it is the Lapp who is the wizard, sometimes the Finn. But the old chief seems to have been extraordinarily silly, from our modern point of view. Not in believing in the magic, but in not realizing that it might be used both ways. Surely if the wizard were powerful enough to cast a sizable spell on the chief's enemy, he would be powerful enough to bewitch himself into freedom and his erstwhile torturer to his death.

The Lives of the Norse Kings is full of such accounts, all of course long before Christianity. And even when primitive animism began to die out in Scandinavia, and ancestor worship and Odin worship began to take its place, the belief in the magic of the Finns who remained animists still continued among the Finn's neighbors.

Thus a ruler of Uppsala named Vanlandia married a Finnish wife. He left her, promising to return in three years. Ten years passed. The Finnish wife consulted a witch, who first caused Vanlandia to yearn to return to Finland. But his companions recognized this yearning as nothing more or less than the result of black magic, and persuaded him against it. So, since he would not return, the witch then caused him to be trampled and then choked to death by a nightmare, invisible to his attendants.

It is in Finmark (Norwegian Lapland) that King Harald meets the beautiful Gunhild, a Norse who has gone to "learn witchcraft from two Finns who are the cleverest men in Finmark." The account makes them seem more like wonderful trackers and hunters than wizards. But we are told that she cannot get away from them without putting sacks over their heads and calling up the king's men to kill them. However, Finnish (or Lappish) magic was still potent, even after the magician's death; next night there came so heavy a thunderstorm that the king could not sail away with Gunhild.

Bad weather was very often blamed on the wizards. King Olav, who later became St. Olav, raided Finland, and had everything his own way until he tried to return to his ships. Then the Finns, bored with his heavy-handed missionary work, sniped the party with arrows, causing heavy casualties as they passed through the forest. When Olav reached his ships, leaving many dead and wounded behind, his troubles were not yet over, for, "During the night the Finns, by witchcraft, made bad weather."

There is, in the *Heimskringla*, plenty of other impartial evidence to show that a little less than a thousand years ago, Finland was famous for its wizards and witchcraft as other countries were for their gold workers, or farmers or fishermen. Herman Melville, writing in *Omoo* as late as 1847 says, "It is a circumstance not generally known perhaps, that among seamen Finns are regarded with peculiar superstition. For some reason or other they are supposed to possess the gift of second sight, and the power to wreak supernatural vengeance upon those who offend them. On this account they have great influence among sailors." Perhaps their ability to control the weather added also to their reputation among seamen.

There is also a record of a student in Abo University who, in the early part of the eighteenth century, was burned alive for having made a pact with Satan. The reason for the belief in this pact was that he had learned, and then managed to impart to some of his fellow students, the Latin language in so short a time that he could only have been aided by the devil himself. To us this accusation sounds suspiciously like an attack of professional and professorial jealousy on the part of one of his teachers.

According to the old shamans, the sorcerers of ancient Finland, there is a magic power in words and in words alone. In the *Kalevala* the man who knew, and could use with the proper routine, the sacred words, could perform miracles of magic; he could command the obedience of the wind and water, of rocks and trees and beasts as well as of humans. Hence perhaps the strong interest even today of the Finn in words, in books and printed matter. Hence also the rapid growth of literacy and the Finn's love of legality, as well as his desire to live under a written constitution.

In the old days there was widely practiced a form of combined song and poetry called runes. These runes were sung or chanted to the accompaniment of a five-stringed harp, called a kantele, a sort of zither. The singers sat in couples, one facing his opponent or partner and the two clasping hands. The leader of the team chanted the first line of the rune, a line of eight syllables, which started the theme of the story-song to follow.

His opposite number then chimed in with the second line,

which must develop the theme, with a wealth of elaboration and alliteration.

The runes were invariably in the Finnish tongue. They floated about the country, repeated over and over among the peasant folk at festivals and weddings for no-one-knows how many centuries. Then came Elias Lonnrot. He was the son of a drunken village tailor living in Hameenlinna. He was ambitious, he loved his country and its people, and out of this love began to grow his collection of legends, charms, riddles, marriage hymns and funeral dirges. He had to learn Finnish to do this, for like many educated young men at that period he had been taught only in Swedish; Finnish was a mere peasant tongue, almost forgotten by the Swedo-Finns who formed the main government of the country.

He got a job in a chemist shop so that he might attend the university; he also played the flute. With enormous enthusiasm and single-mindedness young Elias began to tramp the countryside during his summer holidays, collecting and making notes. With his flute tied to his coat lapel, he tramped and played his way from door to door through the provinces of Karelia and Savo, and as he went he sang whatever songs he had already picked up.

In return, the old men of the village, listening, would be stimulated to sing to him the songs they recalled. One old peasant with an astounding memory kept Lonnrot taking notes for two whole days and part of a third.

Up to the nineteenth century no Finnish literature had appeared. In 1548 Michael Agricola, a Finn who had been a pupil of Martin Luther, had preached in Finnish instead of the accepted Latin, and had translated the New Testament into that language. In 1766 a Finnish dictionary was compiled by a professor at Turku University. There had been little besides.

The first edition of the *Kalevala,* a mere 500 copies, appeared in 1835; a year that later was to be considered a milestone in the nationalist movement. But it was twelve years before this small edition was sold out. In 1849 Lonnrot published the second edition, at a far more favorable time, and its success was overwhelming.

Suddenly the Finnish nationalist movement discovered this heritage of poetry and song in their native tongue. For generations Finnish had been a dying language, fit, it was felt, only for peasants. Swedish, being the tongue of the Swedo-Finns, the landowners, teachers, nobles and prosperous merchants, was also the language of courts, used in all legal matters, and was the only language taught in the elementary schools.

In 1831 a group of young teachers and scholars formed themselves into the Finnish Literary Society. Among the members was Runeberg the poet and writer, Lonnrot, and Johan Vilhelm Snellman. Few literary men have been so influential in the history of any country. Snellman was not a poet, he was at heart a great nationalist and patriot. He believed, and preached, that there should be "One language, one nation" and that Finnish should be that language. With Snellman the nationalist movement began to gather strength.

It is difficult for us to understand this language division within a country. But it was almost a civil war—it was prolonged and bitter. It had no connection with religion since both groups, Swedish and Finns, were now Lutherans; nor was it a racial struggle, since many Swedo-Finns were of Finnish blood, or even more Finnish than Swedish. At one time or another many Finnish families had taken Swedish names, since under Sweden they had a better chance of advancement.

The collection of some fifty runes, or poems, do not contain a single story, so the *Kalevala* is, at first sight, slightly disappointing. It has no epic theme to compare with the tragedy of Ilium. Comparing it to the Norse *Heimskringla* collected by the Icelander Snorri Sturluson, the Finnish poem suffers again. Its people roar no battle cries; no long black keels carrying hot-blooded, cold-hearted warriors are driven to the far-off shores of Constantinople or America's Vinland. The *Kalevala* is a collection of fairy tales, rather unmotivated fairy tales, based on the half wonder incited by imagining the improbable or the impossible. They lack scope, they lack the impact of personality upon human personality; they utterly lack plot.

But as a national treasure the *Kalevala* has a basic importance that is impossible to overestimate. Songs which have brought back the soul to a people who, through the centuries, have suffered everything but annihilation cannot be lightly dismissed. They have more than the appeal of a rallying song, or a national anthem; they came as a revelation to a people who had never realized that they had a history of their own, apart from Sweden or Russia. The *Kalevala* is wholeheartedly and utterly Finnish; something that belonged to the Finns and to no one else. As such it has an appeal beyond measure.

The stories have grown up through the centuries; the earlier ones undoubtedly date back to pre-Christian time Finland. But Christianity had begun to creep in. Pohjola, probably Lapland since it is located in the chill and foggy north, is referred to somewhat smugly as the "land without a priest, the country unbaptized." But the ethics and the whole pattern of thought of the poems belong entirely to shamanism, to the days of sorcery and magic.

Shamanism, which is based entirely on the magic power of words and spells, is a far more primitive form of belief than the mythology of Egypt, Greece or Rome. These latter belong to a period when man had already become a protected and obedient subject or citizen and expected a leader and the discipline of leadership in religious as well as secular matters. The Greek gods and the gods of old Norse legends may even have echoed early legends of tribal leaders; Odin was almost certainly a real king who became a god. Man usually shapes gods after his own image, so the deities were endowed with human attributes. An Odin, a Jove or Jupiter is a leader, a master, a father; he aids the worshiper with good advice if the worshiper gives him good service and asks favors in a suitable manner, as a courtier would ask and receive help and advice from a chief or a king. The god in return expects flattery, promises of reform, and copious gifts.

But the Finns, in the days of the creation of the *Kalevala* heroes, had not evolved to tribal leadership. Any cult of the leadership type is utterly foreign to the poems. Here religion is sorcery pure and simple, a mixture of medicine and mechanism. A man, such as the singer Vainamoinen, "wise and steadfast," is adept in magic, he is not the servant but the master. He never invokes a god or a being more powerful than himself. But he develops tricks, which we would call magic, to permit him to control not only other humans, but other creatures, bears, birds, foxes, wolves, and even trees and stones and water.

To the shaman, the believer in the power of the word, *things* are not set apart from *humans* by the fact that they have no mobility or no will power. The early Finn does not divide things into humans (with souls), beasts and insects (with minds), vegetable (alive but mindless), and inorganic matter (having no life). He saw no superhuman gods above him, and recognized no unbridgeable gulf between himself and all the rest of creation.

A similar state of religious development existed among the American Indians. They believed in all creation as a whole, with no discrimination, and in the power of magic to control it. This parallel between early Finn and American Indian may have influenced Longfellow when he chose the rhythm of the *Kalevala,* the constant use of alliteration in its unrhymed lines, for use in writing *Hiawatha.*

In shamanism the art of life was to make friends and to influence not people only, but all creation. Vainamoinen summons storms and creates magic creatures to help him. Man was the most cunning form of life, and, like an elder brother, could trick other forms of life to help him. Results were produced by spells and incantations, as we might produce results by chemical or mechanical means. Everything in creation had an essence, a personality. Not merely was there a pine tree, Honga, but a daughter or spirit of the pine tree, Honga-tar. The juniper, Katja, has its personality. Katja-tar and the ash tree Pihlaja had its corresponding Pihlaja-tar. Everything conceivable—water, earth, even colors— had spirits or souls which a magician could use to help himself.

A last faint trace of this outlook has survived almost to the present in the form of childhood spells, in incantation and cursing. But it is difficult for us to picture a life in which this belief permeated every corner of the day and night, every action of the human. It is as though we believed that by a suitable magic verse we could reduce our income tax, or repair a misbehaving furnace or TV set.

Yet to begin to understand the *Kalevala* we must do this trick of mental acrobatics. The poems include many magic runes which one may try out for oneself, though it is quite probable that certain essential ingredients have been omitted, purposely, from the secret formulas! More practically it gives one a new viewpoint on the heroes whose deeds are herewith chronicled.

To our eyes these heroes seem unheroic. They may be strong or courageous, but this is only incidental. No swords clash, no noble deeds are done, as among the Greeks and the Vikings. We find it difficult to get wildly enthusiastic about them.

In the beginning Vainamoinen spends eight years floating, storm-tossed, on the seas. He is picked up in a boat rowed by the Lady of Pohjola, and given hospitality. She exacts a ransom from him which only the magic smith Ilmarinen can make. So he sails home by magic, "calls up his cunning" and creates a gold-tipped fir tree with a gold-breasted martin in its branches. He tricks Ilmarinen into climbing up to catch the martin, raises a whirlwind and has him blown away to the distant land of Pohjola to work for the lady and construct the sampo, a magic mill of enormous size which can grind out corn, salt and gold at the same time—that is, "prosperity." This is to be Vainamoinen's ransom.

The smith finishes the job and returns home. Then Vainamoinen has a new plan. He and the smith row back to Pohjola, apparently economizing, for once, on magic transport, and are pursued by the Lady of Pohjola in a boat with a hundred rowers and a thousand warriors. When hard-pressed, Vainamoinen casts overboard a piece of flint and a piece of tinder which by magic become a submerged rock on which the pursuers' boat strikes and founders and all is lost, except of course the Lady of Pohjola. By magic she flies like a lark into the yardarm of Vainamoinen's rowboat. The contest in sorcery starts again.

This is only one of the many stories contained in the *Kalevala*. But in all of them something, to our mind, is lacking. Is it the Christian ethic of the triumph of good over evil, or the warrior's ethic of the triumph of valor over desperate odds? For all these tales are only a triumph of supernatural guile against supernatural guile, and there seem to be no rules as to what is possible within this dream country, and what is not. As in *Alice in Wonderland*, it is a child's world where anything can happen, anything is believed in, no matter how fantastic. It is like watching a game of basketball in which the players may use brass knuckles or a knife, or have the ball moved about by magic. Rules may be broken, skill seems unimportant: so for us, the modern reader, the game is worthless.

In a translation it is impossible to judge the *Kalevala*, apart from the stories, as to literary quality; but most authorities agree that it has little. This is not surprising. The runes that compose it are in a simple catchy meter, and are produced, except perhaps for the magic incantations, more or less spontaneously by men or women at marriages and other village festivities. Finland, having no great courts, no great chiefs with courts of their own, produced no bards or skalds or minstrels, skilled professional singers or entertainers.

This brings us back to the important question: Why did this anthology of folk-verse, first published in the nineteenth century, produce such a resounding effect on the Finnish people? Such an effect that, according to foreign observers it "gave a people back its soul."

One reason for this is founded on a fallacy. Lonnrot, who devoted a whole lifetime to making the collection which he named *Kalevala,* was convinced, and by his enthusiasm convinced others, that he was scientifically "restoring" a broken art treasure, as one might reassemble the shattered Portland vase or fragments of a Ming masterpiece of pottery. His view is no longer accepted. The *Kalevala* was a creation more in the nature of a mosaic whose individual parts had never before been associated.

But for a long time his idea took hold. Here was an epic, age-old, forgotten in its original form, and—surely by magic—being made to live again. And here was a people, the Finnish people, so badly shattered by Swedish and Russian domination that their very language had almost vanished from the earth. The parallel could scarcely escape even a casual thinker. A people hungering to be restored accepted the "restored" epic as a part of themselves, and as a symbol.

The importance of this symbol continued to grow in the years that lay ahead. The Finnish land, but never the Finnish spirit, was broken and rebroken by Russians, then again by Russians and by Germans. But the *Kalevala* was a phoenix which could rise from the very ashes of its death.

And so, by implication, could the Finnish people. The *Kalevala* was the poetic flowering, the rediscovered soul behind the resolute sisu.

The Finnish people are today Lutherans, and devout Christians. But this should not blind us to the appeal of magic which runs through Finnish poetry. A hero in a small row-boat, with only two companions, pursued and on the point of capture by a craft with twelve hundred men, by means of sorcery and magic wrecks and drowns his pursuers.

How often must the Finnish people, in the Second World War,

cracked between the might of Russia and Germany, have felt the need for such a magic?

They produced it, by what seems a miracle. Yet how much of the magic lay in the character of the Finnish people, and how much did that character draw strength from the runes of the *Kalevala?* Who can tell?

5

From Chanted Rune to
Enchanting Blueprint

MOST OLD WORLD capitals have evolved, year on year, century on century, down through the mists of the ages. No one can tell in exactly what year Rome was founded, no one knows the age of lovely Paris, or by whom London was first settled. But Helsinki's birthday and its beginning were the result of a plan; and she has been a planned city ever since that day.

The Finns have never allowed things just to grow, to develop, to happen; for Nature, as it were, to take its course. The Finn, as a human, is master of his universe, as he was in the not-too-far-off days of shamanism. Magic runes have turned into statistical tables, draft legislation and blueprints, but their purpose is the same: to give the new political shamans control over bricks and stones and mortar, forests, trade, economics, and even over the private life of other Finns. The right runes, the appropriate incantations, can accomplish this. The past holds little of interest for him, for it is no longer controllable. But the future—ah, that is another thing!

Finland's survival seems almost a superhuman feat, enough no doubt to convince the Finn that he is the true master of his fate and that clear planning and indomitable will can accomplish miracles, now and in the future, as it has done in the past.

The origin of her capital city is recent, as Old World cities are reckoned. Back in 1550 the main port of the duchy of Finland, then a province of Sweden, was Abo, now called Turku, on the southwest coast. The duchy's governor lived there, government was administered from Abo; it was all conveniently close by sailing ship to Sweden, just across the Gulf of Bothnia. But it was a little too out of the way of the increasingly important trade route between Sweden and Russia.

Gustav Vasa, who had recently united the provinces of Sweden under his rule, took a look over the map of Finland and came to a decision. On the southeastern shore lay a small, unimportant fishing village of a hundred families or so. Across the Gulf of Finland, almost directly south as the king's finger drew the line, stood the Estonian town of Tallinn. From that town the efficient Hanseatic League was carrying on a very profitable business with Novgorod, in Muscovy to that east. Since the days of the Vikings, Sweden had fought many wars to protect her trade rights with the Muscovites.

A good port in the duchy of Finland, nearer to Novgorod, would allow a route to cut directly across the Baltic trade route of the rival Henseatic League; closer also to Russia, it would be less open to attack by Baltic pirates. Another point which Gustav considered was that such a port would be able to load munitions and supplies for the ships carrying men-at-arms to Europe, to fight in the war then going on with Denmark and Germany.

So the citizens of Porvoo, Tammisaari, Rauma and Ulvila were commanded to pack up their goods and chattels, abandon their fields and forestlands, and move down to the selected site where, on the river Vantaa, the inland waters met the sea. The city of Helsinki was decreed.

But a blueprinter like a rune-maker may carelessly omit an

essential part of the magic. The site was too far inland and proved unfavorable for the deeper draft ships then being built, so the town did not flourish as a port. Some ninety years later, in 1640, Per Brahe, the most enlightened and far-seeing of Finland's Swedish governors, ordered the town to move again. It was shifted to face the sea directly, where it lies amidst an archipelago of islands today. The old area forms the present Kruunuhaka section of the city.

The success of this new Helsinki in competition with the Hanseatic League created a new problem. Free merchants from Germany, Holland and Sweden, barred by the closed corporation from Tallinn, poured in and settled; and, more adroit traders than the Finns, began to pile up fortunes, then return home, taking their gains along with them. This was bad for the country. In the end, Johan III of Sweden issued an edict to prevent foreigners from thus abusing Finland's hospitality. All such merchants, departing for good, must leave behind them one third of their fortune.

So the town prospered and spread out, inland from the harbor, though not without the usual setbacks of the period. Like other wooden-built towns of the seventeenth and eighteenth centuries, Helsinki was swept by disastrous fires. Then the Black Death, ravaging northward from the Oriental ports on the Bosporus, wiped out half the town's inhabitants, not an unusual occurrence where bubonic-bearing rats could find countless unsanitary holes in which to breed. But a similar destructive fire in Abo, the capital, destroying almost completely the university library as well as many of the government buildings, did Helsinki an unwitting service.

In 1812 Nicholas I, tsar of Russia, having cast a jealous eye upon powerful Sweden, annexed Finland, and, like Gustav Vasa before him, consulted a map of the country. Might it not be as well if the capital of the newly created Russian duchy of Finland lay a little closer to Russia and a little further from the rival

Scandinavian country? If it lay in Helsinki, in fact, instead of in Abo? It would be easy to claim that the loss of the priceless library and the destruction of the university building at Abo were the reasons for the move. With a twofold purpose but a single edict, it was decreed that the University of Abo be transported to Helsingfors (Helsinki). And with it, all the government offices of the capital. Again a monarch had decreed the fate of the city.

Once more a fire swept the wooden town. This time the re-planning of the old seaport was given to a famous German-born architect, Johan Albert Ehrenstrom. Moving through it, square by square, house by house, he rebuilt it, entirely of stone. The new city far surpassed its former glories; the central section of Helsinki still follows the architect's plan.

The city still stands on the north-south, east-west crossroads of trade. There are several ways to reach it. You can arrive by air from any direction, in which case you land at the airport, well outside the town. It is very like other modern airports, convenient, antiseptically clean and so uninspiredly efficient that you will forget it five minutes after you and your luggage have been put aboard the bus that speeds you to the city. Or you can come in by road, or by railroad. Though the railroad, State-owned and as spic and span as a new kitchen, enters the fine new station of which Helsinki is so proud, rail travel, like air travel, is much the same the world over.

Helsinki is still a port, and turns her most beautiful face to her original love, the Baltic Sea. So the best way to get your first glimpse of the city is by water, for there is no more magnificent harbor in all northern Europe than this White City of the North.

You steam in through a natural cleft between two high walls of bare granite, which made it one of the best guarded harbors in the world at a time when defense from the air was still unthought of. The inner basin is so vast, so deep, that several combined fleets, of the old days, could have found shelter there. Friendly fleets, though, for they would have had to enter single file, through that narrow gut guarded by the bastions of the fifteenth-century Suomenlinna, Finland's fortress.

From the harbor you face the town, brilliant in the morning sunlight, ranged out along the water front, dominated by the golden globe of the Russian cathedral, which reminds you how close Finland lies to the Iron Curtain. The gleaming, onion-shaped cupola is overlaid with pure gold leaf, the newer buildings beyond it are red-roofed, but to left and right the older roofs of the city glisten whitely. The story goes that once a Russian empress, visiting Finland, noted how beautiful were its snow-covered roofs—perhaps she was homesick for those in her own country. She requested that thereafter all Helsinki's roofs should be perpetually white. Well, it's a pretty story, and you can believe it or not, as you choose.

At South Harbor, where your ship docks, a city market mingles the produce of sea and land. Here in open stalls along the cobbles old women and young come in from the country roundabout to display their wares. Fish, freshly caught, compete for attention with gay bunches of sweet-smelling flowers, wild berries from forest and roadside, vegetables so scrubbed they could be popped straight into the kettle, and mushrooms in every conceivable shape and color, to make your mouth water. There are great bunches of twigs, too, leafy birch bound into whisks, which seem a bouquet of decorative greenery for the living room, till you remember that such birch whisks are a part of the *sauna,* the Finnish bath.

Then, with the sound of the noon bell, as though obeying the tap of a magic wand, the market vanishes. Women, carts, baskets, trays, unsold fruit and flowers, all are gone; stalls seem to have melted into the earth. A cloud of blue and white pigeons and a few gulls, asserting the conflicting claims of land and sea, descend to scavenge. Half an hour later the hosed-down cobbles, steaming with wet, are spotlessly clean and awaiting tomorrow's market.

Whether an Oriental bazaar, or Paris' Les Halles, or London's

Covent Garden, there is no place which gives a traveler a better introduction to the character of a people than a daily market. Going from the alien territory on shipboard to the artificial segregation of a hotel the visitor's first impression, however brief, of the Helsinki waterside market will stay with him. It is likely to be warmly favorable. Nobody quarrels, nobody screams, nobody is importunate. Despite the appalling death and mutilation rate of Finland's wars, there are no beggars. Though wealth per capita is still small, the stalls are overflowing with high-grade produce. Everything is fresh and clean and orderly. It is even a little self-consciously respectable; and this introduction of Helsinki and Finland is no piece of tourist board stagecraft or civic face lifting.

Inland from the harbor you follow the wide, tree-shaded esplanade. Two parallel rows of shops and houses face each other across the block-wide grassy park. At one end a fountain tosses its shining waters, at the other a fine open-air restaurant is alive with cheerful noonday voices and the busy scurry of black-uniformed, white-aproned waitresses. Among the greenery and gay flower beds children, as blond and scrubbed as Christmas angels, feed the pigeons from small bags of dried peas; clerks and shop girls, pausing here in their noon hour, bask peacefully on a park bench, eyes closed, faces upturned to the precious benison of the short summer sunlight. In the old days, under Russia, this esplanade was reserved for the ruling classes. Russian officers in shiny high boots and pale blue gold-laced uniforms ogled the pretty girls who carried twirling sunshades, and wore huge hats and summery frocks. Matrons in lilac silk and old men in spade beards and high silk hats exchanged gossip of the European courts in half a dozen languages. No common folk, in those Russian-dominated days, were allowed in the park.

Like all Finland's parks, this has its full quota of statues. Among the maidens and nymphs that lurk in the lilac shrubbery Johan Ludwig Runeberg, the Bobbie Burns of Finland, sculptured by his son Walter, strides in dark stone, an oddly gigantic and formidable figure to represent the gentle poet. The plinth bears in block letters the first verse of "Our Land," the national anthem written by Runeberg.

> Our land, our land, our native land
> Oh let her name ring clear.
> No peaks against the heavens which stand
> No gentle dales or foaming strand
> Are loved as we our homes revere
> The earth our sires held dear.

You ponder on the anomaly of a song written in Swedish for a Finnish-speaking people: Runeberg knew little Finnish. But as you turn eastward into the main shopping street of Helsinki—*katu* means street—you will note that signs at street corners, names above shop fronts, and even the price tags on window displays are all in two languages, Swedish as well as Finnish, the two always side by side. You may be able to puzzle out the Swedish, which at least is pronounceable, but the Finnish will utterly defeat you.

No one knows where the Finnish language began, though it belongs to a group called the Finno-Ugrian, which is still spoken in a part of Russia along the Volga, and is distantly related to Hungarian. Some experts claim that the Lapp language is also kin to it. The language isn't an easy one, and up to a hundred years ago it was dying out, confined to the peasants and to back country districts. Swedish, by law, was used in courts and schools. Then came the period of Russification, when Russia tried every means she could think of to impose her language upon the people. It became a requirement that all pupils should study Russian for seven years. They attended the classes, sat in sullen silence, and with true Finnish obstinacy departed with no single word of Russian in their vocabulary—but with a newborn passion for their own neglected tongue.

Today Finnish has come into its own, and since World War II German has been discarded as a third language study and English is taking its place. Swedish is still required. It must be difficult for Finns to master English unless they speak it early, for their own tongue has no articles, no genders, fifteen cases, and completely disregards the letters *b, c, f, q* and *w*.

It is not hard, in reading a Finnish map, to remember that the once Swedish Abo is now Turku, that the Swedish Tammerfors is now Tampere, and that Helsingfors is now Helsinki; but names of objects in common use are more confusing. Self-service elevators, for instance, bear a label that reads *vestibul,* which is Swedish. But in Finnish the name is *alas.* The bank where you go to cash your check is marked *pankki*—one is inclined to set *hankki* in front of it. The railroad station gets a little harder with *rautatiekirja,* and in Helsinki, should you visit the Old Town, you would twist your tongue around *vanhakaupunki.* The University Botanical Garden bears the formidable title of *yliooiston kasvitieteellinen puutarha,* and most grandiloquent of all, the Finnish Tourist Association is the *Suomen Matkalijahdisty.* But don't worry, there is always a translation in Swedish alongside the Finnish, and if you can't puzzle out that one either, every second person speaks excellent English, at least in the large towns.

Helsinki is not a gay or smiling city; one would never call it jaunty or debonair. As Gustav Vasa in the beginning designed it for usefulness, so it has continued along the same pattern, a city planned for one purpose—to make happy healthy citizens— but with a distinct air of no-nonsense about it. Yet the gay flags that flutter all day in front of the hotels give the somewhat too businesslike streets an air of movement and color; hotels display the national flag of each registered guest. The flags are taken in at night, save on Midsummer's Eve, when the sun remains above the horizon for thirty-six hours.

The shopping district is very much like any American street of fine stores, more American than English. This is especially true of Stockmans, where you can buy almost anything you find at home, and the girls at the counters are extremely pretty, very blond, and speak perfect English. It is difficult to believe that you are in a foreign city, though there are few places that boast such a wealth of fine bookstores. Stockmans book department is the best in all Europe. But then Finland is a bookish country, there is almost no illiteracy, nor has there been for two or three hundred years—another point in which the Finns take pride.

A short walk beyond the shopping center and you enter a noble plaza, handsome with flower beds. All around rise fine new buildings, the national theater, the yellow post office, a grand new hotel. In the center of them all rises the railroad station.

Helsinki's proudest landmark is her station. It was built by Eliel Saarinen, and architects come from all over the world to study it. All the taxi drivers know its fame and the fame of its architect. Of dark reddish stone and brick, the great clock tower dominates the dignified open plaza, but the four gigantic lamp-bearing figures across the front of the building seem to stand grim guard on departing travelers, as though to demand "Is this voyage really necessary?"

As in any place so planned, one misses the charm of the accidental. Do not search Helsinki for the picturesquely antique. There are no ancient buildings, no crumbling ruins nor twisting narrow lanes and alleys. Helsinki was never a walled town, cramped behind high bastions, moat-surrounded. She boasts of being as up-to-date as Chicago—in fact a little more so—and far, far more scrubbed. You can sit in spotless white on any park bench and rise without a smudge on your garments; no scraps of loose paper blow about her wide and almost aggressively clean streets. No lines of washing, hung to dry, disfigure her back alleys: she has no alleys. The Helsinki housewife washes and dries electrically in machines furnished by the landlord. No noisy children play in her busy streets; they play games, mostly planned games, in green shaded parks and playgrounds set apart for this purpose, and paid for by the taxpayer. There are no shabby dwellings. If the householder does not paint his own, and in colors prescribed by the city planning committee, the city will do the job for him and send him the bill.

Around Helsinki the new apartment houses, each very much like its neighbor, are so planned that the taller ones, of eleven stories or so, are built on the heights, giving them still greater prominence. These are interspersed with lower, two- and three-story houses which sit in the hollows. Southern Finland is so exceedingly flat that the city planners have wisely taken advantage of what variety there is, and used the slight slope of ground to give an agreeable variety to the countryside.

Though flowers and indoor plants play a large part in the life of the Finn, one sees few outdoor flower beds, and no smooth, mown English-type lawns. The grass is left uncut, to grow rank and tall and wildflower-filled, as though Finland, with so short a time for them to bloom in, does not begrudge brief life to a single flowering weed.

One cannot explore Helsinki in a single day, nor in a single chapter. The Olympic Stadium belongs in the chapter on Olympics, so you'll meet it there. The city must not be judged on preconceived ideas as to what a visitor expects to find in an Old World capital, but only on whether it has achieved its purpose. And here there is no room for doubt. It is as neat, as comfortable and well planned as a modern apartment; as functional and efficient as an electric kitchen. Alas that efficiency and romance have never gone hand in hand!

Since it is also planned that the Finnish youth shall have a healthy body, sports play a very large part, even in city life—especially swimming, bicycling, running and skiing. There are many fine bathing beaches within easy bus distance, all city-owned and city-administered. There are at least a half dozen park swimming pools, one for men only. The winters, though dark and long because of Helsinki's northern latitude, are not so bitterly cold as in our Montana, Wisconsin or New England. The city is so planned that a half hour's ride by bus or bicycle can take the whole family out into the country, for summer picnics or winter skiing.

Shops and offices close promptly at four o'clock. There are long week ends, and in summer bicycles stream out along every road. Girls with gay skirts aflutter in the wind, boys laden with pack baskets of picnic food for a full week end of meals, whiz past every corner. Along the waterside of Helsinki as well as on water-bordered Tampere and Turku, small sailboats raise their white wings and small outboard motors start up with a happy *gulp,* to *putt-putt* out into the harbor and off to a tiny summer cottage which almost every family owns. Finland boasts of more outboard motors per capita than any other European country.

At night her docks lie empty and silent; at seven in the morning or even earlier the tide of boats sweeps back again, bringing returning commuters. Ole Evinrude, the Henry Ford of the outboard motor, was an immigrant boy who left Scandinavia for America only seventy-five years ago. His invention has come home to bless his fellow Scandinavians.

If, after all this abounding health and planned cleanliness, you seek the old and picturesque, take a bus out to a small and pretty island connected by a long bridge with the town. It is called Seurassanni, not difficult to pronounce. Here have been assembled, among the granite outcrops and tall pointed pines and rough uncut green grass, houses and churches, huts and shelters in an open-air museum of ancient Finland. Here, gathered from north, east and west you'll see a group of old farm buildings, red-painted, of gigantic logs, hand-hewn and dating back to the fifteenth century, or a well-built and charming house built for a minister in the eighteenth century and looking ready to move right into today. There is a kirk, a wolfpit, a prison, a crofter's hut and even a tar pit and a small shelter housing a Viking-type boat.

Each is tended by a caretaker in the costume of the province from which the house has been brought. The buildings are all of logs, and even the early ones are two-storied, for the Finns practiced fuel economy even though they had ample firewood. In the large kitchens, which served also as living rooms, the scrubbed floors are of enormously wide boards; the board walls display gigantic copper pots and kettles; the big soapstone fireplace, three-cornered, to throw its heat well out into the room, seems like the rest, built to function for a family of giants, or for a gigantic family. Some of the beds look oddly modern since they are double tiered, set one above another as children's beds in a large household are today. They seem to contradict the implication of a tall family, till you learn that their five-foot length is due to a custom of early days, when the sleeper reposed propped almost upright with many pillows, surely a most uncomfortable position in which to slumber. It is difficult to imagine one of those tough early Finns suffering from insomnia and having to sit up all night.

Wandering through those ancient houses, room by room, and looking back through the centuries, it is not difficult to people them with the ghosts of their departed owners, farmer and fisherman, parson and lumberman, and their meek or shrewish wives. (Some of the Vikings took to sea to escape the sharp tongue of a nagging wife. It says so, right in the Norse sagas!) The sword marks on the pole that holds the copper kettle in the ancient kitchen tells of the bridegroom who brought home a bride to the household and whacked at the huge kettle beam to show her his prowess in fighting; the huge illuminated Bible in the parson's house tells us of long readings from the Word, and probably the long prayers that followed, with children wriggling on their knees, and the dinner growing cold on the table.

In an ancient shed, down by the water front, two black-tarred longboats rest quietly, their life on the ocean wave long past. One is of twenty-six oars, of the size called *skuta*. They are not unlike the Viking ships shown in the Oslo Museum, but without the dragon prow that signifies a warship. In the later days of their raids on England and Ireland and the Frankish coasts, the sea wolves of Norway and Sweden often hired "foreigners," Finn shipwrights, to do the building for which, as successful warriors, the Norse had no time. The pattern of these boats, with their graceful lines, still persist into modern times.

Working with wood is an inherited skill with the Finns. Now and then they even become heavily playful with it. Outside the ancient church stands a queer wooden figure, crudely shaped like a man, life-sized, painted in gay and now faded colors. A huge padlock dangles from the creature's iron belt. Does this perhaps represent some strange type of Iron Maiden, some barbaric form of punishment?

No, it is an alms box, for collecting funds for the poor of the parish. The lifelike guardian with his oversized padlock was merely a jest of the workman who made it.

A trip well worth the effort is the one by boat, out through the lovely archipelago beyond Helsinki and the castle ruins of Suomenlinna to Porvoo (Borgå). The ship glides in and out through winding waterways so narrow that at times she seems to be cutting a fresh channel between the narrow wooded shores. Along the way there are countless summer cabins, tiny rough bridges, little sandy pathways that twist and wind between the shadows of forest birch and pine and wild pink heather to the summerhouse at the end. These cabins are perennial, they bloom each spring with the first warm weather, and with the first killing frost of autumn are boarded up for the long dark winter months.

It was from Porvoo in 1550 that Gustav Vasa wrenched fisherfolk and farmers, lumbermen and tradesmen to help settle the newly planned town of Helsinki. The deserted town was resettled, and today it has an almost medieval charm. The steamer docks gently in the harbor, where its red-, yellow- and green-painted houses seem to rush down the steep banked streets straight to the waterside. A cobbled road meanders uphill to the old gray cathedral at the top. This was built in 1418; the town, according to tradition was first founded in 1346 by a Swedish king with the peculiar name of Smek.

But the town is famous for more than its Old World charm. Here is where His Imperial Majesty, Alexander I of Russia signed the Finnish constitution, which was to give Finland, for a few years, the semblance of the freedom for which she had fought and bled for centuries. And here in Porvoo is buried Finland's equivalent to William Tell, marked by a modest slab of granite inscribed: *Eugene Schauman, d. 16th June 1904.* He shot his country's tyrant, General Bobrikov, and then turned the gun on himself.

More even than these the little town owes its fame to being, for many years, the home of Johan Ludvig Runeberg, Finland's national poet.

Here, at the age of thirty, Runeberg came to lecture on Roman literature in the Borga Gymnasium. (Finland used the German meaning of this word, which is "a school of the highest grade, preparing for the university"; so he taught a kind of high school.) His life was quietly happy, uneventful and untraveled, save for a single voyage to Sweden. But his writings occurred at a crucial period in history, at a time when Finland was breaking loose from her long Swedish heritage, and the great nationalist movement was gathering strength. Some of his poetry dealing with the war of independence in 1808 was a valuable link between the Finns and the Swedo-Finns.

Today, save in Finland where his "Our Land" is the national anthem, his writing is almost unknown, and even the spirit of that stirring song does not stand up well under translation. His house is preserved as a shrine, just as he left it, even to the coat and hat on a simple peg in the hallway, and the living room furniture which his mother-in-law gave the young couple when they moved here in 1877.

You return again to Helsinki, capital of Finland and perhaps

There are more than sixty thousand lakes in Finland, many of them joined by rivers, facilitating navigation.

A view from the sea of the market place in Helsinki. The selling of most foodstuffs is forbidden for hygienic reasons, but in the morning the sale of fruit, vegetables, flowers and fish is still allowed.

No schools are more up-to-date than those provided
by the Finnish government for the children of today.

Paavo Nurmi, holder of thirty-seven Olympic records for Finland, is a constant inspiration for her young athletes today. Behind him soars the Stadium tower.

The ancient castle of Olavinlinna, one of the greatest in Europe, as imposing today as in 1475, when it
guarded Finland from Russia, just across the border.

Finland is grand country for swift, cross-country
skiing. The Laplanders invented the ski.

Beyond the Arctic Circle. The midnight sun, photographed each hour for five hours and at the same level above the horizon.

In remote villages tiny Lutheran chapels
keep alive the religious spirit of the people.

All along the lakes tiny saunas (bath houses) snuggle among the white birches

A mural, illustrating a scene from the *Kalevala*.

One seldom sees the lovely peasant costumes any more,
save at a country wedding or dance. These are peasants
from the beautiful lost province of Karelia.

Picturesque old farmhouses of trimmed logs, painted red with white bordered windows, can be seen from the train. But Finland is becoming more "modern" every year, and these may not last much longer.

Farm buildings more typical of the countryside today.

A Finnish Laplander in his reindeer fur trousers and four-winds cap. White reindeer are rather rare.

Timber transported in the Vaaksy canal.

The picture above shows the influence of ancient
Finnish architecture on the very modern church at
Salla. The older one is a medieval church at Sibbo.

the most blueprinted city in the world. What impression will it give you as a parting gift when you leave?

To a social planner and efficiency expert it will seem, and truly is, a stupendous accomplishment for an impoverished and war weary people, bowed down by all but intolerable burdens. To a traveler of less specialized interests it will seem puzzling.

For something is lacking. The magic wand has been waved and here for a moment is a town and here are people going about their everyday lives. Yet it is never quite real. They have sedulously hidden their past behind their present, and they value their present mainly for the future that will grow out of it, so that they, like their surroundings, seem blueprinted; planned, not born.

They have no visible roots. Their past is segregated to Seurassani outside the city, so that it may no longer affront the modern eye with reminders that their ancestors lived without plumbing and electric washing machines. Even there, the well-cared-for buildings look a little apologetic, torn from their natural settings and transplanted.

As the door of the plane closes, you may be forgiven for feeling that the brief play has ended and the curtain fallen. The actors, the men without a past until they took their calls, will vanish, and those realistic sets of railway station, airport and apartment houses will be struck and carted away.

Or was it all Finnish necromancy?

6

Many Races

THE OLYMPIC GAMES, that great international contest of athletic skill and prowess, so perfectly suits the Finns that it might have been made to order for them.

Once in four years, wherever these contests take place, the people of Finland are roused to such a pitch of enthusiasm as could not be matched in any other country in the world; an enthusiasm that mounts and mounts to an almost religious fervor. Finland's athletes, like patriots on a battlefield, seem so inspired by their sacred national mission that they are able, when ordinary strength is waning, to call upon that persevering and obstinate will to win, which makes a man forget pain and fatigue, and even peril to life itself, so that he stretches his strength to the ultimate limit for the victory and glory of his country.

The original Olympus was the mountain home of the ancient gods of Greece. The original Olympian games were contests among the gods themselves. Jupiter wrestled with Saturn and cast him forth from Olympus; Apollo vanquished Hermes in a race and Ares in a boxing match. It was in honor of these mythical games that the temple and stadium of Zeus was dedicated at Olympia.

The Marathon race, chief of all the Olympic contests, has a more easily verified historical background. Darius of Persia sent an army to capture and enslave Eretria and Athens. This was in 490 B.C. Hippias, a former and hated tyrant of Athens, led the

Persians, and Eretria, after a long siege, was taken. Hippias then landed at Marathon, a plain some twenty-five miles from Athens.

Among the Greek soldiers one man, Pheidippides, was chosen for his strength and courage to seek the aid of Sparta. For two days and two nights, without rest, he ran, swam rivers and climbed mountains to reach the city. There he told his story, and Miltiades, leading the Spartan army, swarmed down to slaughter the Persians and save Athens. Flushed with victory, the Athenian generals dispatched Pheidippides, already fatigued by his long race and his day of fighting, to take the good news to the beleaguered city. He reached Athens, completely spent, and gasped out, "Rejoice! We conquer!" and dropped dead at the feet of the elders. A fine example of sisu!

In the centuries that followed, the Games centered around the Mediterranean Sea, helping to spread Greek culture and the ideal of a healthy and disciplined body throughout the ancient world. But with the passing centuries the celebrations in the temple of Zeus became more and more corrupt; carnivals, routs and circuses took their place. Even the Emperor Nero entered himself as a swaggering contestant. Finally, in A.D. 394, the Emperor Theodosius of Rome ordered that they cease. Later the temples were pillaged by barbarian invaders, and earthquakes completed the ruin of their walls.

Fifteen hundred years later, in 1896, the Games were revived, to recur thereafter every four years. The first one was held in the restored temple of Zeus in Greece, as was fitting. Olympic in the world of sports connotes an all but superhuman contest, something far above the average. All games represented, no matter what their popularity, must be staged with equal care as to the correctness of rules and perfection of setting; whether a dumbbell contest, aesthetic dancing, still-fishing, military riding, mountain climbing or choral singing. But to the average man, and certainly to the aspiring Finnish athlete, the Olympics means track and field events.

Unlike the Latin peoples the Finns dislike bloodshed and death in their sports. They also dislike contests which entail the contact of one human body with another, such as football, boxing and wrestling. Force and stamina are the two qualities most admired—running is the act that most clearly brings out such sisu. Their language contains at least twenty words to express the action of running, and one Finn in every eight belongs to an athletic club. Small though the country is, it contains more than five hundred competition grounds.

In the Olympic Games little Finland has again and again beaten other and far larger countries and come in second only to the United States. In her own country, in 1952, she won third place, with sixty-six points in the unofficial team scores.

But in spite of her many prizes and the many heroes of her games, there is still one figure that stands out above all others. The barrel chest, the sturdy legs and tireless stride of Paavo Nurmi are immortalized in statues all over Finland. The picture of this Flying Finn, this Ace of Abo, was shown on all the posters for the 1952 Olympics; a statue of him in dark bronze is poised at the entrance to Helsinki's stadium, an inspiration for future contenders who train there.

Nurmi possessed the qualities most admired by the Finns: taciturnity, frugality, relentlessness in pursuing a goal. His character first caught the enthusiastic attention of the sports reporters in Paris in 1924, who bestowed many admiring nicknames on him. They alleged that he lived on black bread and dried fish, which is highly probable, as even today that is the diet of the lower-class Finnish workman. They noted that he ran with the untiring regularity of the stop watch on his wrist, which he consulted from time to time to check his pace. They made copy of his poker face, his vague smile, and the fact that he indulged in those "queer Finnish baths that end with a roll in the snow."

It was in the Paris Olympics that the Flying Finn, in two hours, won the 1,500 and the 5,000 meter race, and with little competition save from his own countryman, Ritola. The next day he won the 10,000 meter cross-country run. Finally he was first over the line in the 3,000 meter race, his fourth individual triumph. The marathon, seldom won by a young man, was captured that year by another Finn, a forty-year-old sewing machine salesman named Albin Stenroos. In that year five of the Finnish athletic teams accounted for nine Olympic first prizes.

By tradition the Olympic torch is first set alight in the old temple of Zeus at Olympia. From Greece it is carried, still unquenched, by hundreds and hundreds of relay runners through many countries to reach its goal of that year's Olympic Games. In the year 1952 it crossed from the south to the north of Europe, then over the Baltic to Sweden. (The U.S.S.R., though taking part in the Games, flatly refused to let the runners through a small corner of Russian-held Estonia, which would have saved many hundreds of miles.) The torchlight went on up to the Arctic Circle, and came down through Lapland to Sweden.

The Finns had very bad luck with their first Olympics on home ground. It rained. They had consulted the weather reports and charts for many years past, and had chosen a day that, up to then, had always been bright and sunny. This time it came down in torrents. The red track around the stadium was a sea of mud churned into soup by the march past the reviewing stand. The white shoes and trousers of the American contingent were spattered to the knees as they followed their flag around the track. The Finns, feeling that their hospitality had been at fault, were steeped in Nordic gloom.

Then came the moment for the opening event of the Olympics, the lighting of the two ceremonial fires, one by the grandstand, the other atop the stadium tower, from the Zeus temple flame that had traveled so many thousand miles. It was not known who would carry in the torch, but since Finland was host this year it would certainly be a Finn.

Breathless, all eyes on the gate, the spectators crowded in the stadium waited. Then, coming in through the entrance, back straight, legs pounding in the familiar relentless rhythm, torch held triumphantly high, came . . . Paavo Nurmi.

With a roar of astonished recognition, as one man the crowd rose to its feet. The Finns simply went crazy! The very gods on Mount Olympus might have heard that full-throated welcoming acclaim. Even the Russians were moved, so they say. The audience shrieked and shouted, stamped and applauded for this man, Finland's hero for thirty years, who could still run with the same flawless stride.

He came to a halt before the peristyle and plunged his torch into the basin. Flame shot up—to burn until this year's Olympics should be formally closed.

Then the torch, still alight, was passed on to the second hero, Hannes Kolehmainen. He bounced up the steps to the top of the 272-foot tower with all his old zest and vim, and there lit the second Olympic flame. The games in Finland had opened.

In one of the ancient Icelandic sagas, which date back to 1020, a Finnish runner is mentioned; though with the usual confusion of that period he might well have been a Lapp. "There was from the Uplands a man called Finn the Little, and some say he was Finnish by birth. He was smaller than most and so very fleet of foot that no horse could overtake him. He was before all men skilled in skiing and shooting with the bow. He had long been King Rorik's serving man and had often gone on such errands as demanded trustiness."

It looks as though the Finnish character over the past thousand years had remained consistent; swift of foot, fine skiers, and wholly honest.

Finland, amazing as it sounds, has no professional athletes, and few of her champions and those training for the Olympics have had university education or the formal sports training that is acquired at college. Among her fifty athletes who, up to World War II, had captured sixty-nine gold medals, all but a half dozen came from working class homes; their practice was done after working hours, in their own time and at their own cost.

Nurmi was, himself, a working man, starting as an errand boy at the age of twelve, then becoming a filer's apprentice. After his astounding victory in Amsterdam in 1928 someone became interested in him and financed him at an industrial school, where he became a skilled mechanic. He still kept up his practice and by 1930 held thirty-seven world records for distance running.

Not only is the topnotch athlete unpaid, but he remains the purest sort of amateur. Not for him the athletic scholarships, subsidies, inflated expense accounts and sinecure jobs. Honor for himself, and glory to his club, village or country are reward enough. What makes this possible is that the principle of sport for sport's sake extends beyond the participants into the organization itself. Profits on amateur college games are not used to eke out professorial salaries. No businessman buys up a stable of tennis or football or baseball players as a speculative investment. No syndicate makes money out of a bowl or stadium, for sports grounds belong to the community, and seem to be run on a non-profit basis.

The Helsinki stadium is an example. The money for it was collected by flag days, and its original seating capacity was 40,000. For the Olympic Games it was enlarged to cater to 72,000. (And incidentally all tickets were sold out a year in advance!) The Games over, it was reduced again, the housing for the male competitors being sold off as co-operative apartments, the buildings used for the women were converted into a training college and home for nurses, and furnishings and miles of toweling and acres of sheets were disposed of by auction. No costly white elephant was left to tempt people from the straight path of amateurism. The cutback allowed athletics to be resumed on the old "sport for sport's sake" basis.

The Olympic Games have had a tremendous impact on Finland, so great that it is difficult to measure. As a new nation it was most important for them to feel themselves part of worldwide events, and to win the recognition of the older nations. For this remote, seldom-visited corner of Europe, the 1952 Games at Helsinki were a shop window in which Finland could display her proudest wares, her stalwart men and women, and fear no competition.

Second in interest to the Finns after running is skiing, though to a Finn his skis are almost as commonplace as his shoes. He learns to ski as soon as he can toddle, and all through the long dark winter cityfolk pour out into the countryside for a week end of sport in the snow. Though there are many ski towers dotted about the country from which jumpers may practice, the landscape is so flat that competition has developed more along the line of racing than ski jumping. The Finns have won most competitions in this corner of the field, but admit that medals for the long, soaring flight down the ski jump have gone largely to athletes from mountainous countries, such as Norway, Sweden, Canada and the United States.

The Lapps are credited with the invention of skis, and there are skis in one of the Scandinavian museums dating back twenty-five hundred years; some of them are fourteen feet long. Arthur Conan Doyle, author of the Sherlock Holmes stories, saw skiing in Finland sometime in the last century, and brought the sport to Switzerland; from there the English brought it back to England, though English snow is too unreliable to make this a popular British pastime.

As skiing is the sport of winter, so swimming is the sport of the short, bright Finnish summer. The Finns love water and know how to use it; in either snow or liquid form it seems to be their second element. Fountains spray in little parks and in the big public squares; small lakes and big lakes, ponds and bays and inlets mirror the skies. The waters are always clean and tidy, no trash disfigures the green that slopes down to their borders. They are alive with swooping gulls, and the larger expanses are busy all through the summer months with sailboats and canoes, rowboats and fishing craft. Almost always the small vacation house, which every Finn owns, is built on the water; not difficult in a country in which so large a proportion is watery. Perhaps out of this love of the water grew the sauna, which is so characteristically and uniquely Finnish.

The *sauna* is a hot bath; not a steam bath, as with the Turkish bath. The word means both the bath itself and the bathhouse. Every large city has many saunas; each large apartment house has one, even the homes for the aged possess their saunas; a Finn never gets too old to enjoy the Finnish bath. When you travel by boat down a long lake, such as on the trip from Tampere to Aulenku, you'll see that the shores are dotted with little red-painted log cabins hidden among the straight-trunked firs and fluttering birches. Each cabin has a large chimney and a stone or plank walk leading down to the water. The more primitive the cabin, say the Finns, the better the sauna.

The sauna, they will tell you, is the last and most virile remnant of what most of Europe practiced in earlier times, and is more like the active Roman than the listless Turkish bath. First the sauna oven is heated for several hours with a roaring fire of birch or pine logs—they must be birch or pine for the aromatic effect. When the stones of the oven have reached a high temperature the fire is put out and removed entirely; no smoke must remain in the cabin.

The bathers then climb to the high, bleacher-like wooden seats and relax in the dry burning heat. The higher the climb, the hotter the air.

After a cupful of water is tossed on the hot stones, the air is filled with steam. You do not desert the seat on the upper bench, nor yield to the first breath of steam. It is pleasant, and a little determination to get accustomed to it will work wonders. As the intense heat becomes tolerable, the trick is to revel in it. Cast on more water, for more steam, then take up the wet birch branches and slap the body all over, vigorously. The leaves, fragrantly odorous of the forest, are wonderfully refreshing, so is the tingling effect of the swatting. The hotter the bath, the harder the beating, the better the results.

Then for the violent contrast! Rush out and down the stone path and throw yourself into the chilling water of the lake; or, if in winter, into the nearest snowbank. And return to the sauna to enjoy all this once again. Then follows a merciless scrubbing all over with brush and soap, by the bath attendant. But it is the shock between the extreme hot and cold on the body that does the trick. Or so the Finns claim.

A famous Roman traveler of the early days, reporting on the peculiar habits of the Finns, remarked, "This people do of their own desire. It is not a torture imposed upon them!"

The sauna is not a penance. Nor is it exactly a sport, a social pose or a health cult, though it is a little of all of these. All that a stranger can say is that it seems to be as much a necessity as food or clothing. Should you, on some Friday afternoon, encounter a gentleman on the streets of Helsinki nearly hidden behind a large bunch of greenery, do not mistake this for a token of his esteem which he is carrying to his lady friend. No, for they are birch branches, and he is stocking up his lakeside sauna for his weekend guests from town.

In all Finland there are some half million bathhouses, about one for every two families. There is no Finnish literature that does not make some mention of the Finnish bath and its delights. In the *Kalevala* it occurs again and again.

> Annikki, whose name was famous
> Heated secretly the bathroom
> Stones she gathered from the river
> Heated them till they were ready
> Cheerfully she fetched the water
> Broke some bath whisks from the bushes
> Charming bath whisks from the thickets
> Then with milk she mixed the ashes

> And she made him soap of marrow
> And she worked the soap to lather
> That its head might cleanse the bridegroom.

Then follows in loving detail the bath of the bridegroom.

The Finn's enthusiasm for the Olympic Games, for the sauna, even his sisu, doggedness, are not as unrelated as they might seem. They are logical developments of the same characteristic, the cultivation of a disciplined obedient body. For the Finns know it is useless for the mind to say "I will" if the body says "I won't," or "I cannot."

The Finn, introvert and taciturn unless he is part Swedish, is difficult for a foreigner to understand. For this reason his self-expression in indulging in the characteristic sauna, and his enthusiasm for sport have been worth considering in detail for any clues they may afford. The former seems to indicate a hunger for self-discipline rather than self-indulgence. The latter a desire to give and receive reward in honor and not cash. Athletics may become his religion, but will never become his trade.

These national characteristics, so nearly universal as to impress the foreigner, may have far-reaching, even startling consequences. Finland has so socialized and tightly ordered a form of government as to seem to the stranger almost tyrannical in its subjection of the individual to what are considered national interests. Yet the Finn, who has fought all forms of despotism for more centuries and with more desperate determination than any other people, approves the present system. Is this another facet of his liking for self-discipline?

And again, does he trust his rulers because he has good reason to believe that his elected representatives will set honor above profit, nation above self, and long-range plans above the daily bargaining of politics? He is in a better position to judge than we are. If he is right, then the day may come when other nations will send their runners to Helsinki to kindle their torches at the pure flame of honest administration. That will be a marathon indeed!

7

Production and the
Luxury Arts

TURKU, until quite recently, bore the simple name of Abo; you'll find them both on the maps. She is Finland's oldest city, the cradle of her civilization and culture. Here, in old Abo, rose Finland's first fortress, the massive walls of which still loom over the town.

It was on the green banks of the narrow river Aura that Henry, the country's first martyr, planted the cross; and here the Mother Church was erected. This is not the present imposing structure, but an earlier building which the Russians destroyed back in 1318. Out of the ruins of the old arose a stronger and more ambitious church. And so began the autocratic domination of the Catholic bishops, who ruled the Finnish church for nearly four hundred years. The brilliant pomp and wealth of their reigns has never been surpassed in Finland, and it is to the princes of the church that she owes the first seeds of her civilization and culture. The history of Turku was, for centuries, the history of Finland itself.

It was under the reign of Bishop Hemming, in 1354, that the world-renowned library of Abo was begun. A library is always a sign of prosperity, for books are costly and readers require the luxury of leisure. Many merchants from Holland and Germany came to settle here, whose names still survive, among them Horns and Flemings. The Scots came too, though more as adventurers than traders, for during the Middle Ages, Scots mercenaries could be found all over the world. Finland today is filled with Highland and Lowland names: Ramsay, Montgomery, Fraser, Hamilton and Douglas. A head of the Finnish Ramsay family, General Baron Ramsay, was commander in chief of the Finnish troops early in this century; the counts of Hamilton and Douglas are connected by marriage to Finland's nobility. The founders of these houses were, for the most part, soldiers of fortune who had enlisted under Gustavus Adolphus III of Sweden, fought in the Thirty Years' War in Germany, and received their knighthood on the field of battle.

With the Reformation and the beginning of the Lutheran Church, Turku lost most of her grandeur; the pilgrimages to the shrine of the martyred bishop ceased and the church treasures were stolen, or disappeared. A few still remain and you can climb the steep little stairs to the museum in the cathedral gallery to see them. But her most valuable treasure, the gold and jeweled sarcophagus that held the bones of the saint, was carted off to Russia in 1913. It may still be there today.

The church is large, and though lacking in Gothic grandeur, and a little battered and shabby, it holds much of historical interest. Up by the high altar in the small chapel to the left stands the tomb of Karin Månsdotter—Daughter of the Moon. She was a lovely Finnish girl, daughter of a commoner, who was for many years the beloved mistress of Eric XIV of Sweden, and the only person who could control his mad rages. Eventually she became his queen, and when he was banished to Turku castle she followed him. He died of poison, and she was then imprisoned in Liuksila, an old castle on the shore of Kangasala, which, soon after her death, was destroyed by fire.

Another chapel here holds the gigantic black marble tomb of the romantic and beautiful Desirée, who married Count Bernadotte, and came, a queen, to Sweden. The story of her entanglement with Napoleon was the subject of a bestseller novel of a few years ago.

Turku, save for her clean greenness, the cathedral and the fortress is not a pretty town. The surprising width of her streets, and the bare concrete-fronted apartment houses give her an oddly empty appearance. Some of the old wooden houses have been preserved in a far corner of the city; they are much like those in the outdoor museum in Helsinki.

The castle, now partly a museum, is gray, grim-faced and enormous. For centuries it was the defender of Finland; Swedish kings held council here, and it was alternately, or even at the same period, a prison and what the history books refer to as the scene of "reckless revels." One room remains much as it was, the small dark cell where the mad Eric Vasa was imprisoned by his brother, Duke Johan, earl of Finland, who took over the throne of Sweden from his brother. There is also a deep and utterly black oubliette where prisoners, lowered into the rock, were forgotten save to let down to them their bread and water once a day. Many old European castles were possessed of these convenient and economical lockups, and the consciousness of them seemed in no way to diminish the brightness of the "revels" going on upstairs.

Turku was also the site of the University of Abo. But, like most of the old wooden town as well as the bulk of the valuable library, and part of the cathedral, it was destroyed by the great fire of 1827. The fire originated in the house of a town butcher, where a servant girl had set alight a pile of tallow shavings from some recently made candles. A sudden windstorm burst over the town and spread the flames from house to house. A week later the ruins still smoldered. The greatest disaster was the loss of the library, which possessed manuscripts dating from the fourteenth century.

All Finland helped in the rebuilding of Turku, but its most generous friend was Alexander I, who gave the city exemption from taxes for ten years, and sent copious funds for building. Soon after this the remains of the library, and the university, were moved to Helsinki. The town's glories had vanished forever.

North of Turku and well inland lies Tampere, quite a different kind of city. On the old maps it was named Tammerfors; nowadays Tampere likes to dub herself the Manchester of the North. Though why she should consider this flattering, except perhaps to Manchester, is puzzling. There is slight resemblance between that smoky, grimy manufacturing city of the English Midlands and this clean wide-avenued town, with its sense of the sea ever present. Tampere has no seacoast, but in Finland the gulls and the sweet salt air seem always to be close by, no matter how far inland you travel.

This is not an old town, it was founded in 1779 by Gustavus III of Sweden. Later Tsar Alexander saw such possibilities in its location that he decreed that it should be allowed to import machinery and raw materials free of duty.

But the real godfather of this busy little burg was a Glasgow machinist, who came here in 1820 from Moscow. History does not relate what he was doing in Moscow, but the Scots do get around. He set up a machine shop here, which eventually evolved into a cotton mill. Being a Scot, he made it pay. This seems to have started the rush, and today there are over two hundred separate industries in Tampere.

The great blessing of this industrial center is ample water power, so everything is run by electricity. There is no smoke; it is impossible to imagine a cleaner, greener town. Three-fourths of its citizens live in mill-provided houses and work in the mills. The workers who fashion rails and the locomotives to run on them, leather goods, plastics, stockings and vast and countless varieties of paper and paper products, saunter along the charming tree-lined boulevards, dine in the waterside open-air cafés, swim at the municipal beaches. Some of the factories are set in green parklands, others spread out along the foaming rapids that furnish their power. There are no slums; nothing is huddled or crowded. The town lies on the Tammerkoski, between the sparkling Nasijarvi and Pyhajarvi: those names are not so formidable if you know that *jarvi* means lake.

In the summer, with its long, light evenings, the workers pour out by the thousands to the little boats that bob, waiting along the quays, or bicycle up along the jarvi shores where the saunas sprout like mushrooms.

In the parks of both Tampere and Turku there are miniature apartment houses for the children to play in, tiny replicas of the eleven- and seven-story "skyscrapers" of which Finland is so proud. Around these play houses wind miniature roads, each with Stop and Go signs of the local pattern. A policeman on duty teaches the children how to obey them, so that they can get their dose of instruction and discipline along with their candy of play. The Finns are nothing if not practical. There is also, in the Tampere park, a small wood-burning locomotive, like the old-fashioned, big-funneled smoke-eaters on the early American railroads. The children clamber in and out of it as they would on an American merry-go-round.

There is a State theater, a workers' theater and an open-air theater; and of course the art gallery—this one was donated by a goldsmith—and the libraries and museums which exist in all Finnish cities.

In a country barely recovering from ruinous wars and a crushing economic burden of war debts and devastation, such lavish provision of public amenities may seem strange to a visitor, but not to a Finn.

For all Finns love their country. Not just casually, or as a matter of course. They love it achingly, with a deep passionate attachment that spreads itself from north of the Arctic Circle, to

the very shores of the Baltic, then returns to center on one par-
ticular corner of it, which the individual loves above all others.
This is not difficult to understand, for without such deep abiding
affection and loyalty Finland could never have survived war after
war, nor would the Finnish character have persisted as it has.
This national devotion explains why her towns and cities are so
rich in parks and museums, libraries and art galleries. An extraordinary number of these are donations of favorite sons.

The parks, besides being rich in trees, are lavish in statues.
Tampere is proud of the four on the bridge between the lakes.
There is the old favorite, the Finnish maiden; there's a hunter, a
tradesman—to remind one that she was always a trade city. Then,
of all things, there's a tax collector! This is strange until you recall that for nearly a century Tampere was tax-exempt. For a
similar exemption, no doubt our own home towns would be willing to immortalize the Collector of Internal Revenue, and even
the Secretary of the Treasury.

Finland, very art-conscious, is extremely proud of her painters,
writers, musicians, poets and architects. Few nations mention the
arts so often in daily conversation, and every taxi driver is ac-
quainted with the name and background of the designer of the
local skyscraper, who also made the plans for the city park and
who erected the new town hall, or railway station. Many artists
are State-endowed—Sibelius was one—and Helsinki has put up a
special home with studios where painters and their families can
work and live together, and every opportunity is given them to
show their work publicly. Through the parks stride tall black
iron effigies of Runeberg, Sibelius or some other of Finland's
great men; hilltops are often crowned with some war hero; among
the lilac bushes in the parks crouches some shy maiden in gray
granite, perhaps commemorating a victory or an alliance; or just
set down there as encouragement to other sculptors.

Unfortunately they are not all works of art, these statues and
groups, and at times the bosky dells seem overpopulated with

scowling poets, leaping nymphs or heroes of the track. But it is pleasant to see so much national awareness of art and its practical encouragement.

Many of the factories, such as those at Tampere, fashioning textiles and nylon stockings, employ only women. This is not surprising or unusual in other parts of the world. What is unusual is the great number of Finnish women in what we are accustomed to considering "men's jobs." Women whose husbands have died in the service of the railroad are given work as porters and cleaners on the trains, and the prettiest slim blond maiden will shoulder a staggering load of suitcases and heft them aboard. Strolling along a busy city street you glance upward at the scaffold of a new building; there, carrying a hod of cement, or cleaning windows, or painting a sign, goes a pair of blue-jeaned legs, and further up, a bright bandannaed head sports a pair of frivolous earrings. Finland believes firmly in the equality of the sexes; the women get the privileges, but they also carry the responsibilities.

This was the first European country to grant women the vote (Swiss women haven't got it yet), and it may be significant that the oldest Finnish document, proudly preserved in her archives, deals with the protection of women. This was back in 1316. At one time customs duties gallantly exempted from duty the incoming trousseau of a bride; and this may be so even today.

That woman's lot was not always so enviable seems borne out in the lines of the *Kalevala*, dealing with marriage.

> In her father's house a maiden
> Lives like strawberry in the garden;
> But a bride in house of husband
> Lives like housedog, tightly fettered.
> To a slave comes, rarely, pleasure.
> To a wedded damsel, never.

Another rune deals more leniently with marriage; it is advice for behavior toward a new wife. "First year, kind words. Second year, command with the eye. Third year, with a light stamping

of the foot. Fourth year, touch her with the birch rod." What
happens after that the rune does not say. But it well might be
that the light touch of the birch rod would rouse the dogged
obstinacy of the Finnish woman to oppose the dogged obstinacy
of the Finnish man. So, early in history, she began her insistence
on her rights.

Almost every kind of job is now open to women, and out of
Finland's five universities and nine other institutions of higher
learning, with an attendance of fifteen thousand students, thirty-
eight per cent are women. In World War II women first gained
officer status in the army. Their organization is the Lottas,
named after Lotta Svard the heroine of a ballad by Runeberg.
Freely translated the doggerel runs:

> For a pearl in the pathway of war was she
> And a pearl all genuine too.
> Though sometimes laughable she might be,
> More oft was honor her due.

Lotta was the widow of a sergeant in the war of 1809 with Russia. As camp sutler she brought butter, eggs and meat from her
little red-painted log farmhouse to the boys at the front, and was
much loved for her mothering and nursing of the soldiers. At
first the Lottas were a voluntary group, unpaid. In 1919 they
were organized into one group, all women's services being combined, some 72,000 strong. But at the outbreak of World War II
they were enrolled as a regular part of the paid services, under
Civil Guard. Their numbers leaped to 200,000 and included
nurses, cooks, radio and phone operators, sky watchers and so on.
During peacetime the Lottas switch to social services.

Though Tampere, which we visited, is typical, she is by no
means the only electrically powered manufacturing town; there
are many such along the west coast. Here to the coast cities lumber is floated, as in centuries past, down the long rapids-obstructed
rivers from the north. It goes out again overseas, in exchange for

British pounds sterling or American dollars, or for other commodities. Finland's main exports may have altered their shape in the centuries past, but not their kind. Lumber and butter they were in the sixteenth century, mainly lumber and butter they are today. Butter remains unchanged except for packaging, but to make more work for Finnish hands and consequently more money for Finnish pockets, lumber is increasingly processed into fine furniture, paper, wood pulp and plywood; and less is shipped as pit-props and rough building material. The rising cost of ocean freight makes it necessary to cram as much value as possible into every cubic yard of hold or deck space, and this too puts a premium on the processed finished product.

The great export centers were once Viipuri in Karelia, now lost to Russia, and Turku on the west. In the sixteenth and seventeenth centuries Turku harbor sheltered many trading ships from the Baltic states and was a favorite way station between Sweden and Russia. Even earlier, in the twelfth and thirteenth centuries merchants from Hamburg, Lubeck, Stockholm and Novgorod strolled the cobbled streets and did business in the close little dim-windowed shops of the old town. Then Finland began to build her own ships until Russia, debasing her to a mere Russian province, nearly ruined her own grand duchy by exorbitant tariffs. But the broken coastline of thousands of islands and inlets and inland waterways made it easier to impose custom dues than to collect them. Smugglers flourished, as they did later in prohibition days. With Finland's independence legitimate trading was restored again.

Now her agricultural instruments go to both the East and the West Indies; she ships the gay painted product of the famous Arabia porcelain factory to Argentina, Spain and Italy. Skis, which she has fashioned for home consumption for centuries, now slide over the snows of a dozen foreign hillsides. Finland is humming with activity.

Handicapped by a late start in the race with other industrial nations, having little mineral wealth, difficult internal transport, a poor soil and harsh climate, such development would have been impossible but for that sisu. To those for whom the *Kalevala* is a second Bible, there is precedent for the feat. Did not the legendary hero Vainamoinen pioneer in mechanization and industrialization when he had built the remarkable mill which would grind out flour, salt or gold, food or wealth? True he used magic. But it was Finnish magic!

8

Drowsy Old Sentinels

OF FINLAND's great and ancient castle fortresses, four still remain intact. Viipuri, which was in Karelia, was lost to Finland in 1940 when Russia claimed the valuable and beautiful province on the Finnish Gulf. Turku castle, originally built to garrison Swedish troops for the duchy of Finland, still stands. Kajaani and Olavinlinna on the east were bulwarks against the Russians, and the fort named for the canonized Norwegian king, St. Olav, the finest of them all, can still be visited.

The need for such a fort dates back to Viking days, when the Swedish sea wolves, who were also great sea traders, began to expand eastward into Russia. In fact it was the nickname for Swedes which was transferred to Muscovites and gave them their name, "Russ." The Finns called the Swedish *ruotsi*, "rowing-men," especially those that settled in Kiev and Novgorod, and even today Ruotsi is the Finnish name for Sweden.

In 1475 a Swedish ruler named Karl Knuteson had his eye on strengthening his trade route to Novgorod. This route was an old bone of contention with both Denmark and Germany. So he commanded Eric Alexsson Tott, head of a great Swedo-Finn family, to erect a castle on one of the several rocky islands in the Strait of Kyronsalmi, near the Russian frontier.

The huge bulk of the fortress took many years to finish; it

covers a giant rock and needs no moat, since it is completely surrounded by the deep waters of the lake, which never freeze. There is no entry to the fort save by water, and the stone of its fourteen-foot-thick walls was brought piece by piece and under guard from the mainland. Every builder worked under guard.

Tott himself came to an unhappy end, for his family grew so powerful and so arrogant—and so rich—that King Christian II of Sweden, coming to the throne, ordered that his head be cut off. Soon after that the great Tott family declined.

The old castle inventories give us some idea of its original garrison, both in size and importance. Thirteen thousand candles were consumed yearly, and so vast was the number of its inmates that fifteen thousand sheep were slaughtered to furnish them with meat. Great stairways mount up and up, and from the topmost floor of the South Tower, with fifteen circular windows set in the massive walls, can be seen a marvelous view of the surrounding islands. From towers and terraces, turrets and chapels, down vaulted passages to the dungeons, all is grim reminder of the days when a constant guard had to be kept on this borderland between two countries.

On a ledge a hundred feet above the courtyard of the castle, there sprouts a great green ash tree, as famed as the fortress itself. During a time of danger, the people of the district sought refuge within the castle walls. But a Swedish girl of noble birth, who had fallen in love with a handsome Russian officer, plotted to betray the castle to the enemy. She was hastily put out of the way, and during the battle that ensued, her body, tossed from an upper window, lay out on the ledge for several days. From that ledge the ash tree sprung, and though the tree has been several times cut down it always springs anew. The castle, the Finns say, cannot forget.

In 1836, three hundred sixty years after the fortress was built, it had lost its military importance and was taken over by the Finnish Archaeological Commission. Since then it has been used as a historical museum, and the former munitions hall is now used for dances. Savonlinna, the old town with cobbled streets which grew up around the castle, was once the fortress of this District of Savolaks.

The old town has seen many wars. No part of the country has been so often devastated by fire and sword as this. The Finnish poet Runeberg told a stirring story of the defense of Porosalmi in June 1789, when the Savolaks "boys," five hundred strong, held at bay the Russians who outnumbered them ten to one. After seventeen hours, almost exhausted, they were reinforced by the Bjornborg regiment. The Russians, retreating, left over nine hundred dead. The fight had been so desperate that the Finns, having used up all their bullets, tore the metal buttons from their uniforms for ammunition.

Kajaani fortress, further inland, was less fortunate than Olavinlinna. It was built in the latter part of the sixteenth century by Charles IX of Sweden. Its last great siege took place in 1715 when the Russian troops, numbering more than four thousand, stormed the castle. The garrison consisted of only fifty men, and a number of women and children who had fled there from the village. For over a month the tiny castle held out against the assault of the enemy as, by day and by night, a ceaseless cannonade was leveled against the seemingly impregnable walls. In the end hunger forced the surrender; on account of the women and children, the Finnish governor capitulated.

The forlorn little garrison marched out. Enraged that such a pitiful number had held him off for so long, the Russian general ordered that the fortress be blown up before his eyes. Tons of explosives were placed within the castle walls. The night was split asunder by the detonations, which could be heard for fifty miles.

Today the ruin stands just as the Russians left it, two hundred and fifty years ago, its desolate grass-grown walls a monument to Russian fury, and to Finnish sisu.

Punkharju is a shrine of sentiment, without historical association; there is neither ancient castle nor museum to intrigue you. Its appeal lies in its unique position. The name means Beautiful Ridge.

On a rise of land between two lakes the highway rambles for five high, narrow miles. There is no underbrush, the road is bordered by the tallest pines in the world, javelin straight, their feet deep in blueberry bushes and lilies of the valley, their sun-kissed tips rising tier on tier on this, the highest point in Finland south of the Lapland mountains. The island, like a giant water fowl, broods on the blue waters, wings outspread. Around her in the vast peaceful silence drowse other islands.

Beautiful Ridge was chosen long ago for a government reservation. Its motif is Nature, handgroomed and cherished. No trash, fallen branch, nor litter of leaf desecrates the pine-needled pathways, and for nearly six miles as the way winds between high arching trees footfalls are muffled in a soft, fern-bordered cushion. All is so tidy and clean it might have been created afresh for the delight of each new discoverer.

At the peak of the rise stands a monument to Runeberg . . . one sees him represented everywhere in Finland. It seems that he sat on this bit of land overlooking the lakes while writing, more than a hundred years ago, "The Fifth of July," in which he compares Punkharju to the most beautiful woman in the world. Finnish poets are fond of this simile; they even see a likeness between the map outline of their country and a beautiful woman reaching her arms to the sky. It isn't a shape most women would care to have, or many men would admire; but this is why Finland is sometimes referred to as the Maid.

Rovaniemi is the capital of Finnish Lapland, Finland's most northern province. This clean, quiet little town, with its white-painted wooden houses, and broad well-paved streets, has an unexpectedly cozy and homelike appearance for an outpost of civilization so close to the chill Arctic Circle. Its extraordinary newness is explained by its recent history, for ninety per cent of the old town was ravaged by fire in the German retreat of 1944.

Driving in from the tiny airport you pass the silently flowing Kemijoki—reasonably easy to pronounce when you have struggled with the name of the hotel—the Pohjanhovi. *Joki* means river, and Kemi is the seaport on the Gulf of Bothnia where all that lumber goes.

You first see the lumber as you pause for a moment at the bridge. Below the bridge, borne up by the wide stream, the logs, all the same length and all the same size as though manufactured to order, flow silently, endlessly through the sunlit day and equally sunlit night of the summer months. For this is the much advertised Land of the Midnight Sun. And along the southern fringe of the Kemijoki clusters a motley array of tents. The town, besides being a favorite of winter skiers is also a favored summer camp site and the people that come here are as varied and colorful as the size and shape of their shelters; Spanish, Italian, English, French and German, as well as Finns. There are even a sprinkling of gypsies. One sees many gypsies in the Scandinavian countries, perhaps because they escape persecution, perhaps because Finland is so honest a country that no one locks doors. The river is too chill for bathing, but one can row on it and fish in it: though mosquito killing might well be the main sport. The insects are blissfully silent, but no less sinister for that; and they cluster in such clouds that the frames outside the hotel's double windows are literally black with them.

On a little rise above the river, conspicuous in so flat a country, stands the hotel, which was mercifully left over from before the war. But to speak of the Pohjanhovi as being "left over" gives a wrong impression. It is as polished as a new mirror, as up-to-date as the latest in American hostels, even perhaps a little more so. The rooms are big and airy and quiet, with wall-to-wall carpets, pretty drapes, double-paned windows and soft beds. The windows are black-curtained, to shut out the midnight sun after bedtime; but there is a breath-taking view of the river from all rooms. It is like a palace out of a snowy fairy tale.

A short taxi ride out of town qualifies the visitor to say that he has crossed the Arctic Circle. But the most impressive part of this Lapland country is the abiding stillness. The silence, clear and blue, irresistible as a glacier, flows straight down from the North Pole, unbroken by rustle of leaf, song of bird, bark of fox. It is flat, flat country here, with few trees. Any impertinent sound that might threaten the peace is instantly engulfed in the vast northern stillness. It is enormously restful. No wonder that visitors often catch "Lapp fever."

It is more an euphoria than a sickness and is like the emotion felt when looking down from a mountain top, or across an unpeopled desert. First, awe of this inhuman immensity seeps into the little human soul: then, as man is in turn absorbed into something greater than himself, there follows an exaltation of the spirit, and he wishes to remain here forever. That's Lapp fever.

Rovaniemi is a traffic junction for roads in six directions, and channels of logs are also collected here on the tributaries of the Kemijoki. The winter fur market is an important one, attended by buyers from many countries.

But though it is the capital of Lapland, do not expect to see blue-clad, fur-wrapped Lapps and reindeer on every street. In fact you will be lucky if you see so much as one in the summertime. For during the warm months not even Lake Inari, much further north, will show you more than a few old couples left behind to tend the goats and cows and potato patch while the herdsmen have taken their young people and their reindeer to the high fells, where, free of insects, they graze peacefully all summer.

Here the sun, at midnight in July, is a blinding dazzle of light, a cold, lemon-colored disk. Rovaniemi is not quaint, it is not even an especially pretty town; but it has the vital self-respecting air of a place that stands on its own feet, and intends to continue to grow in importance.

Though the Kemijoki is Finland's longest river, it is by no means the only one that carries a constant stream of logs from inland to the sea. In the old days lumber was transported from the northeastern provinces by way of the White Sea, that ancient track of commerce with the Muscovite princes in the fourteenth century.

In the days of the Sea Finns, those skillful carpenters employed by the Vikings, the tar boats used to swirl down the rapids, carrying this product of the piney woods to Stockholm, to England, even later to America. For Stockholm tar was famous throughout the world, and in great demand for the waterproofing and strengthening of ships' ropes and for healing wounds in man or beast.

But the slender, graceful black tar boats are no more. Tar is a by-product of charcoal burning, and the destruction of forest land was proving too costly. Nowadays, with careful government control and reforestation, the forests cover seventy-two per cent of the countryside in pine, spruce, birch and aspen. Of these the spruce is the most valuable, due to a world shortage of the raw material for paper making. Private owners of the Finnish forest are largely farmers, and the winter work on these home woodlots is an important part of the country's economy.

The *Kalevala* reminds us of how far back is this mutual dependence on wood:

> On the heath there grew a pine tree
> On the hill there rose a fir tree
> And the pine had silver branches
> And the fir tree golden branches.

Silver and gold they are today, also, for the Finns. And how lucky Finland is, to have her wealth in her forests, not in mines. For felling trees is an outdoor job; it calls for clean work in the open air, often in beautiful surroundings. The Finns are fortunate to have their wealth so easily accessible.

The cycle of the logging season starts in January. During the next three months the trees are felled and dragged over the snow by horseteam to the rivers. At this season of the year the wood is dry and less liable to carry insect pests; it also soaks up less water in the river, so there is not so much danger of the timber becoming waterlogged. Most of the floating starts when the ice melts, in April or May. Men patrol along the river banks to keep the logs from piling up; balancing out on the churning, kicking logs is a wet, hard job and full of danger, since the upper reaches of the rivers are swift rapids, and it is often difficult to break up the jams.

On many of the waterways the logs are floated down in the form of rafts; each raft has its own crew, which travels with it until a lock is reached, at rapids or powerhouse, when each raft must be taken apart. The logs slide singly down a chute which bypasses obstacles and the raft is reassembled in still water at the lower end.

Lumbering is a craft which resists mechanization, and the swift course of a log from forest to factory reminds one how brief has been the modernization of Finland. Except for an occasional chain-saw and tractor, trees are still felled and trimmed by human muscle and snaked down over the snow to the waterside by horses or oxen. Streams and rivers are cheaper carriers than modern road and rail, and these streams are untamed except for a rare dam and spillway.

Yet within a month or two the log has run its course from primitive forest to civilized city, from ax and rude lumbercamp to the most modern machinery, tended by well-dressed men and women for whom co-operatives and the welfare state provide not only the necessities of life but also what seem luxuries. Medical care, varied forms of cheap insurance, minimum wage and maximum work-hours regulations, high-quality housing, co-operative markets, subsidized theater, music and art. A gigantic inverted pyramid, based, so far as the lumber trade is concerned, on the lone axman and his toiling team.

9

Three Points of
the Compass

TRAVELING INSIDE the borders of Finland costs little in effort, in cash or in time. The people are charmingly eager to demonstrate the marvels of their country, and they themselves are habitual tourists, those from the south exploring the north, those from the east the west, equally determined to leave no ground untrodden, no sight unviewed. The roads are good, and if you travel by car you drive on the right, as at home.

Or you can travel in comfort, even in luxury, by train. The railroads are all State-owned, as in most of Europe, and the cars are as shining clean as soap and scrubbing powder and good Finnish elbow grease can make them. You can rise at night from your double-berthed bedroom, and gaze out through the long corridor windows at the endless lakes and the pine fringed islands under the glow of the midnight sun, or in spring moonlight. Almost certainly, a light at the far end of the car will reveal a porter polishing the brasswork, or dusting the dustless window sills, or cleaning the already shining floor. Since this has gone on all day, it seems hardly necessary to polish at night as well. But the Finn's love of cleanliness is a positive passion. And of course it is part of the charm of the country that one sees no trash, no litter, and that no signs are necessary to remind her people not to drop things around.

Many of the trains burn wood, which is so plentiful, and which explains the odd, old-fashioned, funnel-shaped smokestacks and the neat cords of logs stacked beside every station platform; so tidily stacked and cut to such even length and diameter that it seems not only to have been piled there by machinery, but also to have been grown by a similar mechanical process.

Planes too can carry you to almost any part of Finland, and it is pleasant to take this swift flight north, and return by train to the south, thus achieving a bird's-eye view and a close-up of the landscape, and so gathering general as well as detailed impressions.

This is a quiet land, almost a silent land; the Finns are not noisy at work or at play and they go about their jobs seriously, unchattering, almost unsmiling. The land too is serious, unfrivolous and functional. If you expect to see Sibelius' tumultuous music reflected in the countryside you will be disappointed. That noble grandeur is how the Finn feels about his country, not how he sees it.

The fields are fenceless, the soil is light, but it is all so flat that there is no erosion, no need for contour farming. Small cows stand on the borders of streams, gently chewing their cud, and shallow irrigation ditches divide the land, closely and evenly, so that from above it looks like green or brown corduroy. All farms grow huge crops of potatoes, for that is the countryman's staple vegetable and you may, at a meal, find spuds served in as many as four different ways. They are also excellent winter fodder for the animals. In the endless summer sunlight they grow well north of the Arctic Circle, and since Lapland is weedless, require no cultivation after planting. How amazingly the universal potato has spread since Raleigh first brought it from Virginia to his Ireland estate!

Hay, drying on tall sticks so that is resembles pole beans at home, break the chessboard flatness of the fields. Small red or white houses, with neat mats of spruce twigs at the door, show lace curtains in the shining windows, and rows of flowering plants crowd close against the glass. There is always a sauna attached to the farmhouse, and in country places a newly married couple, economizing, will often build their bathhouse first, and live in it till they can afford to put up the larger dwelling.

This is not a country of gardens. One sees few flower beds and no lawns, and the whir of the lawn mower, so universal at home, is never heard. Now and then you'll see an older house that fortunately escaped destruction. These are of logs, painted red; the roof of turf laid on birch bark shingles, and gay with waving buttercups and daisies abloom amid the grass on an unplanned and unplanted roof garden. Inside the old style house the daughter still sits at the spinning wheel whenever she can spare the time, and mother weaves cloth or rugs at the big loom in the kitchen. Huge doughnut-shaped loaves of bread hang from the rafters, and copper kettles and copper-bound cheese tubs gleam from the shadows. But the high open hearth of the old days has become a modern electric stove.

Small "church" villages dot the countryside. Often these are very small, a mere sprinkling of houses gathered around the church, but the parishes are large, extending over many miles. In the old days the farmer would get out the family sleigh, or the family boat; and all the household, in an aura of Sunday starch, soap and the birch from the Saturday night sauna, went off together. The vessels, called "church boats," often carried thirty oars, and could hold every able-bodied man in the neighborhood, as well as the women and children. In summer they would start in the late afternoon, singing as they rowed throughout the bright summer night. It was a glorious picnic.

Today the bus has taken the place of the church boat or the winter sleigh, but the church is still the center of neighborhood gatherings.

Midsummer's Eve is one of the best of the Finnish country festivals, and is celebrated with dances and bonfires from one end of the land to the other. Every height blossoms into flame, to commemorate the mating of Night and Day, for the legend states that Koit and Amarik, the Sunrise and Sunset, begged the Lord of the Sky to grant that they should be eternally bride and groom, and once a year they clasp each other in their glowing arms.

It is only at these country festivals, and then as a rule among the older folk, that you will see the old national costumes. It is a great pity that they are not revived; Finland is almost over-anxious to be "modern." They varied widely from province to province, but the bright clear colors, red, blue and yellow, were general and gay with embroidery. There was the tall cap of lace and feathers worn by a bride in Ylinkiminki, and the fetching little green cap, lace edged, worn by the Aland Island girls. The skirts were long and voluminous. Dresses of cloth that was hand-spun and hand woven were durable enough to justify such pains-taking embroidery. The men wore knee-breeches, with shoes of birch bark; these can still be seen on the national costume dolls in the souvenir shops. There were fine silver belts, family heirlooms, from which hung purse and knife, aprons in brilliant stripes, and heavy silver necklaces that had been handed down for generations from mother to daughter. The coachman type of coat, and roll-brimmed felt hat from Jaskis seem inspired by some early traveling English milord.

Travel today is so easy and so pleasant in Finland. The young people go away to school and, speaking several languages, visit the Continent. And there is far more mingling of one province with another than there was a generation or two ago. Hence the distinguishing characteristics of each province are rapidly dis-appearing. Karelia, poor lost Karelia, annexed by Russia in 1944, was the gayest and most lighthearted, in spite of her centuries of tussle with the Muscovites; Lapland is still given over largely to Lapps and retains more of her old character than most other districts. Though a Lapp may turn Finn it is seldom that a Finn takes up residence in land north of the Arctic Circle, or embraces the hardy Lapp reindeer economy. In the southwest, which is old Finland, the Swedo-Finns more closely resemble Swedes than Finns, in temperament and appearance.

North of Oulu, in what was once called Ostrobothnia, lies Bothnia, the largest of Finland's seven provinces. Its boundaries in the north are Lapland and the Arctic Circle, eastward lies Russia and the White Sea, and to the west the Gulf of Bothnia and the Swedish coast.

This enormous province is a land of endless forests, marshes and roaring rivers. Once it lay at the bottom of the sea, and even now, year by year, it is thrusting upward so that old men recall that, in their younger days, they set out nets where now there is grazing ground for cattle; and from villages that two hundred years ago were lively little ports, now they have to walk miles to the anchored boats. North of Oulu, where many rivers empty into the gulf, was once the great outlet for the tar boats. Here in the harsh land, orchard fruits do not ripen. Once seals and whales were plentiful, now they have been overhunted. But salmon and other fish teem in the white waters of the streams and attract ardent fishermen from as far away as Scotland and the States.

The peasants here are a fighting race, who, a generation or so ago, were accustomed to draw a sharp knife at the slightest excuse, a knife carried dagger-fashion in a leather sheath attached to a wide belt of hammered brass. The pride of the young man was the notch marked on the knife blade, a sign of how much steel he could bear without flinching, as his companions thrust their weapons in the least vulnerable part of his anatomy—a game that often proved fatal.

The Finn on holiday prefers, not surprisingly, to travel by water, his abundant and favorite element. For Finland means fenland, and her countless lakes and rivers are linked by an elaborate network of steamships and motorboats, large and small. Silverline diesel ships, spotless, almost as elegant as a Mississippi steamboat, and the smaller ones that skitter through the lakes, dodging beneath overhanging birch, and pausing at countless little bridges and sauna cabins to take on a passenger or two, are great fun. The seats are wide and comfortable, there is always a snack of coffee and open-faced sandwiches being served somewhere on board, and there is generally someone who speaks English, even if only a seven-year-old who has learned an English poem in school and is delighted to demonstrate his new achievement.

There is often a running travelog, broadcast from the bridge in Finnish, Swedish and English. This is a recorded lecture, which pops off like a chime every fifteen minutes, the captain or some-one aloft acting as disc jockey. It keeps you informed of what lake you are now passing through, a little of its history, what the schedule is, and often statistics of production or of the exports and the figures connected thereto. The Finn dotes on figures of any sort, and especially those dealing with finances, which he recites like magic runes.

From May to October these spic and span little boats dart back and forth throughout the network of sparkling lakes and rivers, gay with a friendly rivalry. Water lilies bob along the banks, an angler fishes quietly in still waters, children rush out from a red log sauna, splashing lustily to catch the wake of the boat. Girls in bright skirts and sweaters come out to wave; they look as mod-ern and as smartly dressed as any camping group at home. The air is clean and tangy, and life tingles with excitement. No wonder the Finn adores his country with so singlehearted a passion.

Finnish food is excellent, if you like it finny. For in Finland you cannot hope to escape the fish. You may choose, from snack-bar or menu or smorgasbord any number of dishes that resemble pie or patties, cutlets or creamed something-or-other; but when you dip your fork and taste the first mouthful, ten to one, no *fifty* to one, you've got fish on your plate. They are all good, but they are thirst-provoking as so many are salted or dried before cooking.

The restaurants in the city and in the de luxe hotels that dot the land are all excellent, as fine as you'll find anywhere in the world, and invariably immaculate. No matter where you go you'll find this sparkling spotlessness, even in the ice cream stalls and little lunch bars. Don't be afraid to try them. Their open-faced sandwiches will be fresh and as pretty as a still life, with dots of minute pink shrimp, and little paper-thin cucumber slices curled about a dab of salt fish or radish, and the most delicious butter. For the Finn understands butter: it is one of his chief exports and even if he serves you margarine it will be so butter-perfect you can't tell the difference.

There are flavored porridges—a favorite lunch dish—and cloud-berries, rather like a large-seeded white raspberry, served with thick cream (even their name is delightful); and cranberries on fried bread, known as poorknights. The pastries are wonderful to behold, the beer cold and delicious. But everyone in Finland drinks milk in enormous quantities. Tea drinking is not in favor, it is too reminiscent of Russia; but coffee is taken with every meal and at odd moments during the day, quarts and quarts of it. The ice cream, sold at little kiosks on the street, is as good as you get anywhere.

But don't expect to be able to pick up a meal at odd hours; Finland is too systematic and methodical for that, and the drug-stores don't boast a lunch counter throughout the length and breadth of Finland. Breakfast, called *sami aamiatnen,* is served up to the hour of ten a.m. Then the tablecloths are whisked away, and should you glance into the dining room you'll see not a soul, unless it's the usual cleaning zealot polishing the already gleaming floor. Lunch, called *lounas*—and that's fairly easy for a Finnish word—is strictly from twelve to two. If you are in a hurry, grab a plate and fork and hie to the cold table, where the smorgasbord is spread to whet your appetite. You'll have as many as fifty delights to choose from.

Dinner, the big meal of the day, is called *paivallinen,* and is served until seven, but in the cities you can still order à la carte up to midnight. Such a belated meal, however, will surely mark you as a foreigner. The Finn is an early riser and must organize his day so that he can cram into it all that he can make it hold. He works hard, he plays hard, and you can bet that he sleeps just as hard. For there is a cheerful purposefulness in all that he does. Phoenix-like, a nation has risen again from the ashes of the past, and is racing through the present into a still more promising future.

10

North of the
Arctic Circle

PERHAPS the most interesting corner of Finland, and certainly the most unusual, lies north of the Arctic Circle in the provinces of Petsamo and Inari. This is the land of the Lapps. Lapland stretches eastward from Finland into Russia, and westward across the top of Sweden into Norway, where it is called Finmark. Here, preserved, as it were, in cold storage, may still be seen a way of life that was old and traditional long before there was any Scandinavia, Russia or other historic country, and that still transcends the boundaries of all four states.

For the Lapps are to the Finns what the Indians are to the modern American, though unlike the American Indian, many still follow their tribal customs, wear their characteristic dress, speak their own language.

The origin of the Lapps, the "Banished Ones," and their strange stone age culture is lost in the snow swirl of time and the icy Arctic mists. It is known that they came from Asia, crossing the Karelian Isthmus many centuries before the migration of the Finns, and were later driven northward by the Finns themselves. But long before them came the reindeer, and before even the

102

reindeer there must have been the reindeer moss, since the three—moss, deer and Lapp—are completely interdependent.

The first wild Lapp hunted the wild reindeer. Then the dog was domesticated and the hunter saw the wisdom of trying to control those wild herds—and himself became domesticated. Out of this developed many things; the hunters' feeling for right of ownership, his skillful use of the lasso to catch and earmark his own beasts, his invention of skis on which to pursue and protect his herds. As he began to possess more personal property than he and his family could carry, he trained some of the deer to haul and carry for him, as man further south was beginning to train the horse.

But even nowadays the reindeer is still half wild. The herdsman cannot herd the deer to any place he himself chooses to go; they cannot be restricted in their grazing and penned like cattle. For the deer feed almost wholly on the sparse moss and lichen. It is this growth, which flourishes only in the far north, that dictates where the deer shall graze; the deer in turn dictates where the herdsman shall move, in one season and another. So that, north of the Arctic Circle, settled villages are almost unusable, save briefly, during the dark winter months. A family of five needs two thousand deer for bare subsistence, and such a herd may require up to two hundred square miles of this specialized grazing.

Here then, in the land of the midnight sun, live the Lapps, who call themselves *Samieds*. They are short, hardly more than five feet tall, with pleasant, alert features; sturdy, immensely courageous and hardy, since only the fittest can survive the Spartan life they lead. Their life is as specialized, as untouched by modern civilization as any on earth.

Everyone knows what a reindeer looks like; in story books, and on Christmas cards it is portrayed more than any other animal. But no one knows how those "eight tiny reindeer" got into the Santa Claus picture. St. Nicholas—in America we use the Dutch form of his name—was a bishop of Asia Minor back in the third century A.D. Centuries later he became patron saint of Russia. To further scramble available information, the sled he drives is not a reindeer sled, not Lappish at all, but came into Russia via Poland—which had never, within historic times, so much as seen a reindeer. The good bishop, the sled and the reindeer are unlikely ever to have encountered each other in real life.

The deer, even without Santa Claus, is sufficiently striking. Both male and female have horns, great branching antlers which they shed once a year, and which, with their heavy shovel-like hoofs, are most useful for digging through deep snow to the moss beneath. A deer can shovel through a three-foot fall of snow, and can sniff the moss at an equal depth. During the winter, when the deer cluster round the winter cabins of the Lapps, they plow labyrinths in the snow so deep that only the tips of their horns protrude. The fawns follow along behind, shoving their elders out of the way, or even running beneath and prodding upward, should an adult deer uncover a particularly succulent bit of moss.

In the spring, as the snow begins to melt, the winter Lapp village is a busy place. For as soon as the crust forms on the snow, the deer will be off on their annual stampede to the high mountain meadows, the fells where the does will calve and where the whole herd can be free of the insect pests that, with warmer weather, begin to plague them relentlessly. In the turf and log houses blankets are rolled, the oval birch bark boxes are packed, household cookpots, all so constructed that they can be stowed easily in baggage sleds or on reindeer back, are in readiness, and the sleds stand, ready to hitch, outside the door. Pack and draft reindeer, selected and trained for strength and docility, are rounded up and confined in the corral.

Suddenly one morning the night's frost has formed a crust on the old snow. The deer are off. And the herders race behind them.

With wild yells and much barking of dogs, the men channel the herd, though they may string out for all of ten miles. Behind them, amid a flurry of snow and the jangle of bells, come the women and children in the lurching, bumping reindeer sleds. Here too it is a game of follow-the-leader, for the beast in the leading sled is trained and old and wise, the strongest deer of the herd. He wears a bell on his bright red and yellow collar; a single rein attached to the base of his horn leads back to the small, canoe-shaped wooden sled. He wears no bit, but is guided by the rein, and the sled is partly steered by the heavily booted feet of the driver dragging in the snow.

Behind the leader in a long string follow the other migrants, children packed in cradles on deer back, or riding atop a deer, the older folk in sleds running beside; each deer is fastened to the sled or the deer ahead, the end animal acts as a sort of brake on the downhill grades.

There is little rest on this trip north—perhaps a half hour halt for a small fire and coffee—since now that the herd has started, there is no stopping them. The herdsmen on skis, each with a dog or two at his heels, keeps them together. Not a landslide, that black stream beside him, but ten, fifteen thousand reindeer pouring down the last slope to the meadows, moving unhurriedly, at an even trot, like a billowing sea, while the deer's breath, like a cloud on the frosty air, spreads out beside them.

The mountain meadows are reached, the camping place of many summers before, the hearthstones waiting as they have for many years. The herds, insect free, relax, and grazing, spread out. Here at last is the true mountain country for which all winter the Lapps, as well as their deer, have yearned. Here is a horizon of open sky, low snow-clad peaks, sparse groves of birch on the slopes—freedom and space.

The camp is quickly set up; this is a small group of *kata*, large wigwam-like tents erected around the permanent hearthstones. The poles, brought here to this treeless country on deer back, fit closely together, and around them are hitched two long cloths of sacking, with a third to cover the entrance but remaining loose enough for the nose of an inquisitive dog to thrust aside. Around the hearthstone are neatly arranged the few simple cookpots, and the copper kettle for the salted coffee which the Lapp drinks in such quantities.

The main food is reindeer meat, dried or frozen, and made into stew with potatoes and barley meal. All cooking is done over the open fire whose smoke escapes through the open top of the kata. Glow-cakes of barley meal are half baked on the hot stones, then turned to toast in the glow of the fire. Cloud-berries and cheese of reindeer milk add variety to the simple diet. This milk, thickly creamy, is also sometimes used in the coffee, but the deer is difficult to milk and the yield is little more than a cupful at a time. Also the calves need it more than the humans.

Since the Lapps' life is nomadic there are no tables, chairs, beds or other furniture in the kata. The floor covering, renewed once a week, is a thick layer of birch twigs, over which blankets are unrolled for beds, and furs for additional covering. The Lapps prefer to squat or to loll on one elbow as they eat or gossip around the fire.

Of all the people of Finland the Lapps are most picturesque in their costume. The Finnish Lapp wears a long *kufta* of heavy wool in bright blue, embroidered in wools and metal threads around neck and cuffs and often also down the back and across the shoulders. This is knee-length for the men, longer for the women. Reindeer-hide breeches and over them *bellinger,* leggings of fur heavily padded with hay, to above the knee. The moccasins, of brightly embroidered reindeer fur, turn up at the toes and lace with gay red bindings; these are also stuffed with senna hay, as are the gloves in winter. The hay absorbs moisture and can be renewed and dried on the line over the fire before wearing again.

The long coat, a fur *pesk,* is slipped on over the head and held low down on the hips by a heavy silver-studded leather belt, often a valued heirloom; into this is thrust the knife which both men and women carry. Only in their headdress do the sexes vary widely. The woman's cap is of bright red, prettily trimmed in blue and yellow about the face. The "cap of the four winds" worn by the men is blue, and stuffed with feathers, it juts out like a four pointed star, jauntily away from the head; or when old and limp it blows to all the four winds.

Here, in the high bleak fells, guarded by the wise dogs the reindeer browse all day and through the sunlit night. Life moves slowly when, for weeks on end, the sun never sets in this Arctic summer. During the night hours it still lingers, lemon-colored and dazzling at about "an hour's height" above the horizon. No wonder that the Lapp is said to have no sense of time; for where there is no sunrise, no high noon or sunset to reckon by, how can you measure the hours?

A young deer cannot be broken to harness until he is about three years old, but the calves are often given to the children to gentle, so that from the first those intended for pack use or for sled will become accustomed to the human voice, to hand and even to the lasso. Calves can be coaxed to come for a handful of salt, just as a colt will come. And just as the boys and girls play games with the lasso, one of them pretending to be the deer by holding a pair of castoff horns on his head, so they play similar games with the young deer and in time the calf will halt if so much as touched by the lasso.

It is now too that the calves are earmarked. Each herd has its own special brand registered with the government authority. Even the boys and girls have their own small herds and know the deer individually, though they do not give them pet names such as are given to the dogs. A sharp-eyed Lapp herdsman can distinguish ear notches thirty feet away, in a milling herd.

In some of the Scandinavian countries, Sweden for instance, government teachers are sent out to the summer villages to start the children on their three R's. This is a wise system, since any long break in the hereditary culture of this stone age people unfits them for their traditional way of earning a livelihood and means the gradual breaking up of the family. The children, sent away to boarding school as they sometimes are, may return dissatisfied with the simple life of the katas; may lose their skill with lasso and skinning knife, and be unwilling, as among some of our Indian tribes, to return to the tribal customs.

As the short summer passes there is increasing darkness, the sun sinking for longer and longer hours below the horizon. This is a warning, the herds must be rounded up and strays from other herds be sorted out. Though the Lapps work on foot, not on horseback, this is not unlike a Western roundup, with the same wild yells of the herdsmen, the same use of the wise little dogs, the same skillful use of the rope. Then one morning the Lapp family will waken to find their blankets deep in snow that has sifted in through the open top of the tent; a welcome snow, for it is needed for the sleds to run on. With autumn come heavy sleet and high winds, and one morning the crust has formed and it is time to travel south. The spring stampede with baggage and reindeer is repeated, but southward this time, in a three- or four-day's race against threatening blizzard and the darkness of lengthening winter nights.

Now comes the busiest season of the year. Once arrived at the winter village, the deer are corralled into pens. This is their mating season and the bulls are difficult to handle, even dangerous. In milling and stampeding the young calves are often killed and the stronger males, fighting with their great horns, may wound each other seriously.

This is also the time for slaughter and the preparation of winter food and of skins for home consumption or trade with the outside world. Every part of the reindeer is of use to the Lapp. Blood sausage, a mixture of blood (blood prevents scurvy), salt, kidneys, suet and barley meal is poured into casings and boiled for twenty minutes. This is a great delicacy, like the Scottish haggis. So, too, is the marrow inside the bones of the deer. Reindeer-hide supplies skins for garments, leggings, boots and gloves; also coverings for the small canoe-shaped cradles. The sinews are used for thread, horns are fashioned into knife handles. Dried blood stored in reindeer stomachs is hung in the small storage houses high on stilts to freeze, well away from prowling wild beasts and even hungry canines. This is the usual food of the herd dogs; they seldom get meat, it is too valuable.

Lapp houses are simple, as simple almost as their tents, hardly more than an earth floor and a hearth around which the family gathers. The roof, of birch bark shingles and heavy turf on top of that, keeps in warmth and keeps out damp. The walls, of turf, or logs—like our own early log cabins—are almost windowless; there is no space for luxury or privacy. Unlike the Swiss, who have cultivated many skills of carving, watchmaking and such with which to pass the snowy winters, the Lapps are not skilled craftsmen. Perhaps it is the long darkness that discourages handicrafts, perhaps it is the need to be alert for attacks of wolves or wolverines on the herds, or it may be that the nomad life discourages ownership of tools and their products; few nomads are craftsmen. The women spin and weave a little, the men work with leather and wool: "hard" materials are traditionally the man's to work with, "soft" belong to the women.

Even in winter the Lapp women's tasks are not light. Many of the men go to the "outlands" to work, to Petsamo to the nickel mines, or they join the fishing fleet, leaving a few herdsmen to tend the deer. But the women have the children to care for at home as well as the duties of the small potato farm; care of the cows and goats, gathering, chopping and bringing in firewood. Many of them still spin and weave, and almost all clothes, especially the skin moccasins and the reindeer fur pesks, are made at home. There is the curing of meat, the chewing of the reindeer sinews and fashioning them into thread with which the skin garments are stitched, knitting, caring for the dogs, and so on and on. It is still very much a pioneer life, perhaps far harder than for our American pioneer women, since the temperature is usually well below zero and there are two months of almost total darkness to get through.

Unlike most peasant people the Lapps have no folk dances, no traditional music, and no musical instrument of their own, save a small reed pipe made from the dried stem of the angelica plant. A strong religious revival in the Lutheran Church in the last century even forbade music, and, of all things, the vanity of curtains in a window! The old songs were also forbidden. These can still be heard from time to time however. The chants, rhythmic and plaintive, called *joika*, deal with snow, clouds, flowers, storms, the deer and personalities. Sometimes a musical saw is used for accompaniment, and recently tape recordings have been made of these.

The big event of the Lappish year is the Fair, held on the Norwegian border, in Kautokeino, in midwinter. Here forest Lapps from the more settled southerly country meet with the nomad mountain Lapps and with the Norwegian Lapps from Finmark, and others of their blood from the northern provinces of Sweden. They speak much the same language, their costumes are similar in many ways, but the nomad looks down on the forest folk as "outlanders"; renegades who have given up herding as their sole subsistence and now till the fields, lumber the forest and live in settled towns.

The trails to the Fair run crisscross over the wastes, the canoe-shaped sleds plowing furrows like winding watercourses. Along the widest and most frequented trails there are little steadings where men can stop to warm their numb bodies, drink coffee, eat and sleep for a few hours of the long darkness. At the Fair there are races—a deer can travel ten miles in twenty-nine minutes, clocked—and as much swapping of likely beasts as at an old-time fair in New England. Here the young people meet other young people from distant villages. Lights glimmer in the windows and pour their yellow brilliance over the snowy yards; marriages and christenings take place in the small, brightly lighted church, followed by enormous feasts. The Lapp trader can swap his hides and furs for such necessities as coffee, tobacco, salt, sugar and knife blades. And on the long road home under the waving curtains of the Aurora Borealis, sledding or ski-joring behind the newly swapped deer, he can congratulate himself on his latest bargain.

The silence settles down, the great silence of the north that seems to unroll like a deadening blanket, straight from the North Pole. The bark of the Arctic fox, the distant howl of a wolf breaks through for a moment, or one hears the snap and crackle of the Northern Lights overhead; then all is engulfed in cold and still-ness.

This Lapland corner of Finland is a harsh, bitter country. Like a relentless landlord it grants no secure tenure; its tenants, like gypsies, must be ever on the move. They learn no arts, practice no crafts, till no soil, grow almost no crops. They take their orders from the reindeer as the reindeer takes orders from the moss, and the moss from the climate. None but the hardy Lapps could accept such grim conditions—but that is their sole safeguard.

11

Finland Faces
the Future

IT WAS in 1939 that Russia, having walked into
Poland, turned toward the Baltic States and Finland to achieve
her old ambition of turning the eastern Baltic into a Russian lake.
Estonia, Latvia, and Lithuania were swiftly gobbled up and it
became evident that Finland was next in order. Russia, as is
always her technique, demanded and threatened. The demands
were too much for the Finns to accept, but they had the temerity
to temporize before signing their own death warrant as a nation.

Mannerheim, who had saved the country twice before and was
again commander in chief, ordered a partial mobilization, though
it could only postpone the inevitable. War followed. This was
the period known in Finland as the Winter War.

It was headline news, for at the time the Allies were stagnat-
ing at the Maginot line. Finland, with nine divisions, managed
to halt the forty-five divisions of the Soviet army for a hundred
and five days, during one of the coldest and bitterest winters recorded in a hundred years. America sent money for civilian
supplies; Sweden sent arms, but inconsistently refused to allow
France and England to send troops through her country to aid

Finland in her extremity. By the spring of 1940 Russia's overwhelming might broke through the Finnish defense lines.

It had been an epic fight against tremendous odds, in which the gallant Finns are believed to have accounted for nine of their enemy for every loss of their own.

The terms of the peace offer were bad, even worse than had been feared. But they had to be accepted for there was no alternative, as Finland knew. Then what happened next seemed to offer some hope, though it was to result in a worse tragedy; Russia and Germany fell out. Germany demanded help from Finland and a passage through Finland from the north to attack Leningrad. Finland, against Mannerheim's advice, acceded.

To the Allies, fighting Hitler, this seemed treachery. To Finland it seemed the only chance of repelling her age-old enemy and regaining her freedom. It seemed as though Germany might be able to do for her what the Allies had failed to do; Germany had sent considerable food to the starving refugees. Finland, in her need, could not afford to be finicky. It is probable also that her Government, somewhat out of touch with the world and the progress of the war in Europe, did not at all realize how close to collapse was Germany's army.

But with the fall of Hitler, Finland was again wide open to Russian aggression. At the peace conference that followed she expected no mercy—and got none. The Germans, who had entered from Norway into Lapland must, Russia claimed, be driven out. She gave Finland twelve days in which to achieve it. Naturally the Germans refused to go, and dug in. So the Laplanders and the northern Finlanders were themselves forced to retreat. In twelve days some fifty-six thousand took refuge in Sweden; the remainder were driven south.

The departing Germans, carrying out a scorched earth policy, destroyed ninety per cent of Lapland's property, every house and barn was burned, and the market town of Rovaniemi laid waste. Large herds of reindeer were ruthlessly slaughtered. In Finland as a whole every ninth citizen had lost his home to Russian or German invaders.

Nor was this all. Russia demanded, and got, the country's most valuable province, Karelia. She gave the citizens what she considered a most generous choice; they might, she announced, remain and become from then on citizens of Russia, or they might depart, taking nothing with them. Out of a population of four hundred and twenty thousand less than a dozen Karelians elected to remain!

For Finland, with a population of less than half the number of New York City, to absorb these homeless, possessionless refugees, without jobs or connections, seemed well-nigh impossible. In addition there was the devastation of Lapland, nearly a third of the country laid waste. And finally Russia demanded from Finland as the "invader," a reparations bill amounting to eighty per cent of Finland's exports in peacetime. Much of the bill must be paid, not in the country's normal exports, but in machinery and metallurgical products not a normal part of Finland's economy.

At first the Finns felt that it would not be possible to meet these crushing demands. Yet, without a whimper, with amazing cheerfulness, the demands *were* met. And on September 19, 1952, a day of great relief to the country, they completed, exactly on schedule, the last reparations payment. An amazing feat, one that probably no other country in the world could have attempted or achieved.

Looking back it is easy to see that the Allies, in allowing Finland to be so drastically punished for her one lapse from virtue, were playing into the hands of Russia. But at the time of the peace treaty, Russia was still our gallant ally, and Finland was something worse than an enemy; she was a friend who had turned traitor.

We, as well as Finland, now pay for our shortsightedness in abandoning her to Russia's tender mercies. By the terms forced upon her by Russia, Finland is not permitted to make any treaties, whether for trade or protection. This has been interpreted to mean that Finland cannot accept Marshall Aid, join a Scandinavian alliance or the United Nations, or become a member of N.A.T.O. Other ex-enemies may become our friends, but never Finland. Russia so decrees.

But there is one bright spot in this gloom. At the end of the war Finland still owed debts outside the country, one of these—a large one—to the United States for food sent her in 1919 during the desperate shortage caused by the civil war. Payments had been promptly made on this debt, up to 1949.

In America a growing feeling of admiration for this honest little nation led to a movement to cancel the debt. But Finland wanted no favors. Thus began an unusual contest between proud debtor and generous creditor, a most remarkable reversal of the usual international situation.

The delicate handling of the problem was, in its way, almost as remarkable, in these days of tactless blustering and undiplomatic diplomacy. In 1949 Congress voted to accept Finland's request that a certain sum should be utilized to further understanding between the two countries.

The money in fact is to be returned by the generous creditor to the generous debtor by scholarships for young Finnish men and women to study in the States, and for young Americans to teach and study in Finland. Under this exchange program more than a hundred citizens come to America each year, to acquire new skills in universities and scientific institutions, and to study American methods in their chosen field: journalism, city government, labor unions or industrial production. In return they spread understanding of Finland and the Finnish way of life among the Americans.

The results are already beginning to be apparent.

12

Finland's Human
Trademarks

THERE ARE four great names, like human trademarks, that carry Finland's fame throughout the world; there are others, but these four especially. Paavo Nurmi, proving with rhythmic stride and stopwatch on wrist his country's unflagging sisu and self-discipline. Then there is the great Sibelius, through whose music Finland's soul sings to the world. The architecture of the Saarinens, Eliel and Eero, father and son, leaps bravely into the future, inspiring all to follow them.

The fourth name is that of Field Marshal Mannerheim, in his way the greatest of them all. But for him there would be no Finnish athletes, Finnish music or Finnish architecture. In fact but for him there would be no Finland. Three times, when all seemed lost he returned to lead his people. Three times he rallied them to face hopeless odds, and to throw back the overwhelming enemy. No, indisputably—and no Finn will deny it—he is the greatest of all Finland's sons.

Of Nurmi the athlete we have written at length in connection with the Olympic Games. He is the Babe Ruth of his age and country, a well-loved, noncontroversial figure, the epitome of a popular hero.

Eliel Saarinen the architect speaks in a language which may transcend political boundaries, but it is a technical speech, unknown to most of us, and impossible to translate from stainless steel and concrete to ink and paper. To understand his Finnish work without seeing it is impossible, as impossible as to appreciate the music of Sibelius without ever hearing it. Though his most famous work is the Helsinki railroad station, he is better known in America among architects for having won second prize in the Chicago *Tribune*'s great international building competition. It is claimed that his innovations revolutionized skyscraper architecture in the States.

His talented son Eero Saarinen was destined to become even more famous. He was born in Finland in 1910 but lived, a naturalized citizen, in Michigan. His work covered many facets of the designer's art, but probably his most outstanding creation was the newly completed TWA terminal at New York's Idlewild airport. It is described as "not unlike a monstrous prehistoric bird just screeched in to a landing," a creation of metal and glass designed "not to go and sit in" but entirely as a place of transition.

Saarinen's modernistic General Motors Center in Michigan also brought him much fame; it is a delight of lagoons, towers of stainless steel, colored brick and floating stairways. All of his work displays a startling and pleasurable break with the past, his buildings incorporate for instance no nostalgic traces of the indigenous log cabin design, no techniques suitable merely for wood and stone. This may not seem so strange until we recall that even the beautiful Greek temples were blatantly log cabins adapted to the use of stone; it is no easy thing, even in the arts, to break entirely with tradition.

In the work of both the Saarinens there is a brilliant interpretation of the national tendency to ignore the lessons of history, but still, like most of Finland's modern experiments, to remain strictly functional. Perhaps Eliel was even more Finn than architect; Eero, with genius, combined both until his death in 1961.

Johan Julius Sibelius, seems to have broken all the generally accepted rules for genius. Such handicaps as personal suffering, hardship, bereavement, striking against fanatic service and a burning purpose, are most often the sparks that fire a patriotic musical genius. Yet nothing could have been further from Sibelius' successful, well-to-do, middle-class life.

The man known to the world as Jean Sibelius was born in 1865. On his father's side he was wholly Finnish but from his mother he inherited a strong strain of Swedish blood. So, like Mannerheim, he was a Swedo-Finn and was brought up to speak Swedish, in a Swedish household.

From his home, where in the Hameelinna Lyceum he received a thorough classical education, he went at the age of twenty to Helsinki to study at the University Conservatory. Later, aged twenty-seven, he went to Berlin and Vienna to continue his musical studies. It was abroad, separated from his native land that Sibelius' nationalism began to awaken. It was now that the long and bitter language strife between Swedish and Finnish speaking groups was at its height. Though Sibelius had spoken Swedish since childhood, he took a strong Finnish stand; part of this may have been due to the tightening of the Russian grip and the tyranny of General Bobrikov; part of it youthful rebellion, or it may have been his marriage to Aino Jarnefelta, a member of a cultured Finnish family of writers and musicians.

Whatever the reason, or combination of reasons, he began to break with the influence of Tchaikovsky and the German Romantic school that had overshadowed his earlier composition, and to base his work on the heart of his own emotions. Did the language struggle suggest to him the need for a link, in music, the universal language? It is possible.

His first great work is entitled "A Saga," a symphonic poem, an extraordinarily effective composition despite the fact that only one theme is used throughout.

In 1904, while Finland was still under the iron heel of Russia, the composer took his family to settle in Jarvenpaa, near Helsinki, There he lived until his death in 1957. In a pretty and simple L-shaped, two-story house, wooden, white-painted, he worked and composed, and met somewhat reluctantly with admirers and interviewers who came to visit him. For his five daughters, whom he called his "five best symphonies" he built a tiny house like a doll's house apart from the main dwelling, that he might be free of childish noise and play while he was composing. But Jean Sibelius never did his best work indoors; he preferred to pace up and down the garden paths between his collection of peonies, smoking one of his famous cigars, and finishing the work in his mind long before he set any of it down on paper.

Though in 1900 he made a trip to Paris, Berlin, Amsterdam and other European cities, conducting the Helsinki Orchestra in his own compositions, he had little desire to leave home, and made only one trip to America. That was in 1914, where, at the Norwalk Festival in Connecticut, he again conducted. His life was lived very much in an ivory tower of his own choosing.

It is remarkable that, in spite of this self-imposed seclusion and the fact that after 1925 he wrote not at all, Sibelius attained and preserved his stature as one of the great composers of the twentieth century. His fame, outside his own country, was particularly notable in England and the United States. His tone poem, the patriotic "Finlandia," written in 1899, has attained the status of a national classic.

In his symphonic poems Sibelius made use of themes resembling folk music; his subject matter is derived from the wholly Finnish *Kalevala,* whose discovery and popularity came about the time the composer was beginning his musical labors. In his music he captured, and expressed, something of which the Finns themselves were unconscious; but once expressed they themselves felt deeply, as did the rest of the world. This was actually a surge of national emotion, released in music. Many composers have been able to take folk themes and enlarge upon them. Perhaps only Sibelius has been able to go deeper and bring up from the subconscious what his nation itself could not express.

The life of Baron Gustav Mannerheim cannot easily be separated from the contemporary history of the country itself, so closely were the two intertwined. He was born in 1867 of a Swedo-Finn family, and early chose the army as his career. At this period of her vassalage to Russia, Finland was permitted to maintain a small, independent army, the officers receiving their early training in the Finnish Corps of Cadets School at Hamina.

Young Gustav joined the school on his fifteenth birthday. Intensive work and iron discipline characterized the school curriculum, and one night in 1886 Gustav, bored and rebellious, took French leave, or as we might say, played hooky. Forty-eight hours later he was curtly informed that his career in the Finnish army was at an end.

Gustav went to say goodbye to his fellow students, and to inform them that he was off to join the Nikolaevski Cavalry School at St. Petersburg. It was his intention to become an officer in the Imperial Cavalier Guards, of which the beautiful Russian empress was, herself, commander in chief. This calm information was received by his fellow cadets with considerable hilarity.

But a year's very hard work, and intensive study of the Russian language, passed him into the school he had chosen, and in 1889 he graduated among the top dozen of a hundred cadets. And this tall, handsome, debonair young Finnish nobleman became in time a member of the tsarina's regiment. In one of the world's most exciting and cosmopolitan cities he lived the gay, yet hard-working life of the military in the nineties; his memoirs record his pride in his horses, his delight in his colorful gold-braided uniforms and the rigorous elaborate ceremonies of the emperor's court.

As a young officer he went with the Russian army to Manchuria and Korea to take part in the Russo-Japanese War—a war in which the Russians absurdly underestimated the ability of their enemy, and were defeated. In these months in the East Mannerheim learned a surprising respect for the Japanese and their tactical discipline.

Shortly after his return to court he was dispatched by the Russian General Staff to explore and to map certain hitherto almost unknown parts of eastern Asia, on which Russia had already cast a covetous eye. For two years he traveled, via Samarkand, Kashgar, the Gobi Desert and the fabulous Silk Road, names of romance and of danger. This was an undertaking well suited to Mannerheim's character, and was perhaps the happiest period of his life; he was completely on his own; his breeding, courtesy and diplomatic talents made him feel at ease in the highest circles of the intricately ceremonious life of these countries, and he was able to send back to Finland many important scientific records, which are, even today, of considerable value.

On his return Mannerheim was posted with the Russian troops in Poland, then a Russian possession. Here, for seven years, he resumed the lighthearted life of the peacetime cavalry officer, hunting, dancing and practicing maneuvers.

When the First World War broke out he fought, naturally, in the Imperial army. But when the tsarist regime fell he found, in the chaos that followed, that it was impossible to keep discipline, nor could he protect his own officers from the wave of bolshevik butchery that was wiping out all that was of value in old Russia. He wished to return to his own country, but without actual desertion of his post this seemed impossible. Then fate took a hand; he sprained his ankle, seized the opportunity to get permission to go to Odessa while it healed, and so escaped to Helsinki.

In Finland he found his country overrun with Reds. Russian soldiers, who had been garrisoned in Finland, had captured whole towns and villages. There were no organized Finnish troops, and

Mannerheim was asked to take charge of the "White" regiments, hastily scrambled together, and was given the post of commander in chief.

He was then fifty years old, but his life of activity and of duty to Finland was only just beginning. His first move was to organize a surprise attack on Ostrobothnia; with its capture he won valuable and much needed arms for the Whites. For some months the civil war dragged on, ruthless and bloody as are all civil wars, though actually this was a war to liberate Finland from the occupying Russian Reds and their Finnish sympathizers.

Unfortunately, and very much against the advice of their commander in chief, the Finnish Government invited German troops to come to their aid. They seized the opportunity, and not unnaturally thereafter did not wish to depart. It was a situation to be tragically duplicated twenty years later, in the Second World War. Not only did the Finns sign a mutual aid treaty with Germany, who was then fast losing the war in Europe, but granted her the right to establish bases within Finland itself. They also voted to dismiss without any special note of gratitude or award of honor, such Swedish officers as had given up status in their own army to come and fight for Finland.

This was an ingratitude that Mannerheim could not face. His army had driven out the Russians; peace was signed. He departed for Sweden, only to learn that Finland had invited a German, Prince Frederick of Hesse, to become their king. It is an invitation that, today, the Finns themselves prefer to forget.

Britain and France, still fighting Germany and about to recognize the new and independent government of Finland, now withdrew their recognition, since she was about to become a vassal of Germany. Fortunately for Finland, the collapse of the Kaiser's army and his flight to Holland soon followed. General Mannerheim was recalled from abroad and asked to become regent until a president could be elected.

As he writes in his memoirs, "This was certainly one of the

greatest ironies of my life, to be made Regent by the very government whose disloyal attitude had sent me into exile, after the work of liberation completed by my leadership." Other great leaders, Churchill among them, have suffered similar ingratitude, and recall in the hour of need.

Mannerheim was regent for a year, until the new republic could be formed and receive recognition from, and hence trade with, other countries. There followed eight years as minister in charge of defense—he had refused the appointment as head of the army in peacetime—and eight years of racing the storm. More clearly than most, perhaps because of his intimate and realistic knowledge of the Russian character, Mannerheim recognized the dangerous growth of Stalinism, and not only its menace to his own country, but to all the world.

Repeatedly he urged that Finland, Norway and Sweden join together under the League of Nations, in a northern alliance and pact of mutual aid. Repeatedly he urged that Finland maintain a strong, well-organized army, even in peacetime. His warnings were brushed aside as so much nonsense. Norway and Sweden preferred to remain "neutral." All three countries, as well as their neighbor Denmark, and even Great Britian, were pouring their taxes into organized social efforts, schools, hospitals, more and better roads, and government aids and grants of all kinds. They ignored the lesson of the past, even the immediate past, as do most short-memoried democracies.

There is no better example in all history of the adage that history repeats itself. When the Second World War broke out, Russian troops, without provocation, marched into Finland, bombed Helsinki and outlying villages; and Finland was again unprepared. Again she asked Mannerheim, now aging, to take charge. He was once more appointed commander in chief.

The following years are part of Finland's history as well as Mannerheim's and have already been related. Two wars against their Russian neighbors were fought within a term of four years, both terminating in a peace treaty, which, in both cases Russia almost immediately violated. The Soviet government had altered little from the tsarist's.

At the age of eighty, ailing and very weary, Mannerheim was asked by both political parties to take on the position of president as well as wartime commander of the army; he was requested to hold it for life. But he refused, saying only that he would see Finland through her next negotiation for peace. He wanted to refuse the honor, twice offered him, but now at such a crisis, when Finland's independence hung in the balance, he felt that it was his duty, since no one else understood both the Russian and the German mind and background.

So, for a time, Mannerheim received the highest honor Finland could bestow on him. In 1946 he resigned, ill and worn out, and died in 1951.

In the epilogue to his memoirs he strongly advised Finland, and in fact any democracy, to look back on its past mistakes and to profit by them; and warns that any country in the world must keep itself constantly prepared for war, if it truly wishes to insure peace.

Gustav Mannerheim's part in world history can scarcely be over-estimated. In the opinion of other soldiers he excelled in that most exacting art of generalship, the strategy of defense with out-numbered troops and improvised matériel.

To the Finnish people he seems greater still. Three times they scorned and discarded him. Three times, too noble to harbor resentment, he returned to give them fresh hope, and by his inspired leadership to save them from their folly.

Far-seeing diplomat, titled patriot, ablest of professional soldiers, self-sacrificing servant of his people, Mannerheim must be measured by higher standards than the ones we apply to those other great Finns, the athlete, the composer, the architects. Nurmi, Sibelius, the Saarinens exemplify attainable goals. Mannerheim is less, or more, than a popular idol. He is a remote ideal.

INDEX